ERWIN MORTIER (born 1965) made his mark in 1999 with his debut novel *Marcel*, which was awarded several prizes in Belgium and the Netherlands, and received acclaim throughout Europe. In the following years he quickly built up a reputation as one of the leading authors of his generation. His novel *While the Gods Were Sleeping* received the AKO Literature Prize, one of the most prestigious awards in the Netherlands. *Marcel, My Fellow Skin, Shutterspeed*, and *While the Gods Were Sleeping* are also available from Pushkin Press. Mortier's evocative descriptions bring past worlds brilliantly to life.

ERWIN MORTIER

STAMMERED SONGBOOK

A Mother's Book of Hours

Translated from the Dutch by
Paul Vincent

PUSHKIN PRESS
LONDON

Pushkin Press
71–75 Shelton Street, London WC2H 9JQ

Original text © 2011 by Erwin Mortier
English translation © Paul Vincent 2015

Stammered Songbook first published in Dutch as
Gestameld liedboek by De Bezige Bij in 2011

This translation first published by Pushkin Press in 2015

0 0 1

Flemish
Literature
Fund

The translation of this book is funded by the Flemish Literature Fund
(Vlaams Fonds voor de Letteren – www.flemishliterature.be)

ISBN 978 1 782270 21 8

Set in 10.5 on 14.5 Monotype Baskerville by Tetragon, London

Printed and bound by CPI Group (UK) Ltd., Croydon CRO 4YY

www.pushkinpress.com

STAMMERED
SONGBOOK

———

Today my mother gave me a thorough dusting, thinking I was a piece of furniture. Perhaps a chest of drawers or an old cooker. She ran a bright yellow duster over my shirt buttons towards my neck, waved it about around my ears and dusted my chin. Then she motioned for me to open my mouth—stuffed the duster in and forgot us.

She's lying on the sofa, on the rug, slumped back oddly against the cushion. My father says: it's not getting any better. I lean across her face and ask: do you know who I am? She smiles, a faint crease of her mouth, which has become virtually lipless.

She nods. Yes, she says, I know.

And her smile broadens, and seems to pump the lips full of blood, cover her jaws with flesh. Her eyes, which are like tin coins, impenetrably hazy, brighten between eyelids that lose their texture of flaky skin and inflammation and have eyelashes once again. The sunken cheeks become rounded, as if her smile travels through all her limbs, smoothing every wrinkle in her body that is old before its time, and making the happiness of a very young girl come tumbling out through her tissues.

She gets up, claps her hands. She wants to dance.

She waves her arms; I hear her sigh, and in her eyes is the rapture of a child that has only just learned to walk and strolls proudly down garden paths. Then her legs slip out from under her, she scrambles upright—and once more she slides over, and again.

Sometimes she falls into my father's arms, giggling as if slightly tipsy, sometimes backwards against me. I pull her up with my arms under her armpits. Her legs thrash, her soles try to gain a grip on the floor, the back of her head tips from side to side across my ribcage like the disproportionate head of an infant on wobbly vertebrae. Her muscles, those lame strings attached to her bones, tremble, tighten, relax, her breath whines through her body, and her hands with their swollen fingers clutch the back of my hand. My father smiles faintly and looks for a chair to set her down on.

I wake up and realize that I must have cried in that dream.

Death that sits at table here is called Mum. It sits at the head of the table, cloaking both her and us in sorrow, the familiar place that it has claimed for itself for months with her shuffling tread from the front door to the dining room. My mother, the crow with a cold with that one teardrop always on her beak. Our nest, once so fleshy, is a buckled cage with a mechanical songbird rusting away inside.

This is the mouth I gazed at for heaven knows how long in the cradle. This is the mouth whose gymnastics of caressing, whisper and lullaby must have pulled me upright on the slippery surface of words. This is the mouth that is now shedding its language, stripping the words vowel by vowel into puffs of breath, gnashing of the teeth, smacking of the lips. Sometimes she mumbles out mouthfuls of porridge, and it's me who listens and with a handkerchief wipes the mess of words off her chin.

It begins—but when does something like that begin, what signs are the first? It begins with the word "book", the word she just can't think of as she stands looking at my library one afternoon and asks when I'll next be …ing, you know, one of those things, will I soon be …ing another—and she brings her hands side by side, fingers outstretched, and opens and shuts them. Was I going to do it again, that writing what do you call it, one of those things. She gives my father a nudge with her elbow: you say, you know.

I think: I must sit right opposite her, where my father usually sits, and then she'll see there's someone there. Only when I bring my face close to hers, I think, does that stubborn fog in her eyes lift.

I say—I've said it so often recently—do you recognize me? You know who I am, don't you?

And she nods and she laughs, and I ask: did Marc drop in? And she nods again. Yes, she says—the first word for a month and a half. And why did he come by, Marc, on Friday?

She shrugs her shoulders. Don't know, don't know, she says, and her face contorts and she cries.

I take her hand in mine. Why are you crying? You mustn't be sad; we're here, aren't we? And then my father comes in. She follows him with her eyes from the cupboard to the table; she doesn't lose sight of him for a moment.

I think she knows a lot, he says.

I realize that I only write to hear sentences dancing without interruption through my head. To make rhythm, acceleration, rallentando, to make pauses sing. Just to be able to hang from dashes—the trapezes of syntax—weightlessly for a moment from the roof beam of a sentence, I let these words loose. What luxury it is to be able to swing through the rainforests of language from creeper to creeper like a performing monkey.

Or did it begin when she stopped going to the choir? Normally she never missed a Thursday. She said she was hoarse, that her voice was going. Perhaps she realized she could no longer read music, the last "language" she had learned. Was she already ill when she became restless if we arrived unannounced, we, my brothers, sisters and their brood? Her silent panic in front of the kitchen unit, because she couldn't manage to lay the table. The sudden crying fits, usually after she had lashed out at my father. The crying that, I now realize, had to make up for the increasing shortage of words. But at the time we laughed it off. It'll blow over, we said, isn't her menopause finished yet?

How must it feel to see the world around you lose its contours, the whole network of language, language memory, which hangs over things so unemphatically that we only notice it when it develops holes? Does everything become hazy, or does it, on the contrary, stand out more sharply as the unsayable gains strength?

He has become her memory. More and more often she comes in uncertainly, a little closer to him. Her senses are starting to stumble. If she can't get any further than stammering, she looks at him wide-eyed. If the answer doesn't come quickly, there is a hail of reproach. You really forget everything! She moans. And to me: he can't remember anything. It's awful.

What strikes me most about her, what makes me saddest, is the double silence of her being. Language has packed its bags and jumped over the railing of the capsizing ship, but there is also another silence in her or around her. I can no longer hear the music of her soul; the existential aura around her, that whole vibrating fabric of symbols with which she wove herself into the world—or, conversely, the world into her.

I am very sensitive to that whole system, that web, that network, which constitutes our being and which for want of a better designation I still call our soul. It is the subtle poetry, the tragedy, the beauty, the microscopic dread which every concrete life carries with it and in some way is able to emanate wordlessly. People have their own echo; I find it hard to explain. I can sometimes hear the white noise of their existence, the snatches of music—and they sound nice or not and in me too the whole human fanfare reverberates, sometimes harmoniously, sometimes shrilly.

But with her I hear scarcely a thing any more, sometimes the same kind of whoosh that first struck me when I was very young and one night the château was ablaze. I remember looking at the sea of flame and as we got closer was surprised that it did not spread silently. I heard the inferno softly shrieking. Somewhere in those caverns of fire and dense smoke glass burst into smithereens, burning beams whistled, stones cracked, etc. I now hear something similar in her: a faint lament of virtually soundless, all-embracing decay.

He cooks scrambled eggs for her, and lovingly puts the pan on the table. She gives him a look of displeasure and shakes her head, grumbling.

You know I don't like scrambled eggs, she says. I only eat fried eggs.

Fried eggs used to make her gag. She only liked omelettes.

He puts the pan aside, fries two eggs and eats the scrambled eggs himself.

She's changing, he says.

She's becoming more silent every day. More and more tears have to replace the words that have vanished into thin air. Sometimes her lips move, the corners of her mouth tremble, and she produces a short burst of sighing. Then it seems there are still thoughts there, but on different wavelengths, beyond the range of my eardrum. I think of her as if she were an old valve radio, the kind I used to see in elderly relations' houses. I'm thinking of the interference and the snatches of voices when the tuner moved through the frequencies. Sometimes she seems in despair and for a moment her brain seems to be searching: stammering, stuttering, lots of silence.

Her "I" is becoming lost. That "something" that makes people so recognizably themselves. The whole repertoire of habits, ways of talking, sleeping, walking, standing, it's all changing. A kind of hybrid person is being created from traits and behaviour that I can remember as hers, and others which are unknown and perplexing, as if a parasitic consciousness is emerging in her flesh.

And then those afternoons when we sit at table and do our best not to lose patience when for the umpteenth time she gets stuck in mid-sentence. I can almost see the sentences stumbling over her lips. Verbal rubble, grammatical ruins lie strewn around her over the tablecloth.

Yes, that's it, she says each time we finish the sentence for her—as one finishes off a lame horse.

My father looks at me and raises his eyebrows meaningfully.

It's only the beginning, I say while she is in the bathroom. I have resolved never to give false hope, but it feels as if I am gouging a knife into myself and into him, into his melancholy father's flesh.

Afternoons full of the pack ice of silence, ice floes of silence, when I think: if only I could hear her say everyday banalities just once more.

Would you like some coffee?

Are you hungry?

You will be staying for supper, won't you?

Apart from that we do the best we can not to regard the slow death that is taking place at home as an ordeal—which is not an obvious reaction. Rationally I can only hope that my mother won't have to suffer much longer, because it's so pointless. She has scarcely any awareness left of time, place or other people. The flamboyant woman who always liked life and pleasure around her has become a twisted, emaciated figure who shuffles down the garden path to the car, laboriously opens the door and sits in it, presumably because she feels safe in the little Peugeot, that tin womb.

It breaks my heart to see it.

At the same time I find the thought of her no longer being there at all chilling, and I'm also rather concerned about my father, who at present with great patience and devotion is postponing his grief—a suitcase that is becoming heavier and heavier…

Sometimes I am struck by the lack of feeling of my fellow human beings, for example when I hear that it's terrible, of course, but that sixty-five isn't that young any more. As if there's an age at which you can abandon someone to their fate.

We write poems—that is, attempts at eloquent complaints about the whims of fate and destiny, against the structure of the universe and ourselves. But there is no sign of life at the window concerned, while the queue grows longer and longer—and an A4 sheet is stuck on the glass, announcing: our customer services department is never open.

I babysat her for an afternoon. She was restless and sometimes aggressive. She wanted to wander off. My father had gone to watch my nephews play football. I had to bolt the back door.

After a while she calmed down, and then we—I can't call it anything else—"played house", but without the pleasure children get from it. She brought a pair of Dad's trousers from the bathroom. First she wanted me to put them on, probably so I would look like him. Then I had to fold the trousers up for her. She took them over to the table. I had to smooth the bundle for her. Then she wanted to step out of her shoes and into her slippers, and out of her slippers into her shoes, and into her slippers again. Then into bed for a moment—and me on the landing crying, waiting for her to get up again (she always gets up, always, after about five minutes).

Only after two hours or so did she calm down completely. Sat shivering in the chair downstairs. I asked: are you cold?

She nodded.

Helped her into her knitted jacket, and then sat next to her. I rubbed her back, and she occasionally rubbed my belly with the back of her hand.

Sometimes she looked up and fixed me with a searching gaze. It is horrible to detect something in her pupils of the hopeless battle that must be being waged in her head, the dogged struggle, doomed to defeat.

I regularly think: let her die, let her go in her sleep, which is almost never a peaceful sleep any more, but irritable slumber, as if sleep eludes her even in her sleep—like everything else. A year ago she sat on her chair all day long when the radio broadcast Bach, as if the divine order of his music disentangled the knots in her head.

She sat there the whole day, and even held her palm against the speaker. She motioned us to be quiet as she didn't want to miss anything.

How jealous of Bach I was.

Sometimes I dream that you're dead, that I'm standing by your body in which the devastation has taken place, and I don't know if I'm relieved or sad. I just feel a searing pain in my chest, and I think: this is the price of my birthright, the settling of accounts for what was agreed when I fell from your pelvis forty-four years ago, without you or me being involved.

At the party in the garden, among all those people, in the shade and in the sun, you walked back and forth between the tables on the grass, abandoned, uncomprehending. If the hectic behaviour of the playing children and screaming on the trampoline became too much for you, you went into the house, where you stared out of the window. You used to be the life and soul of the party, now you're a ghost wandering through the house. In the afternoon you slept in the deckchair, in the shade of the silver birch, while we ate at a table next to you. We all looked over our shoulder now and then at your sleep, which was peaceful.

Sometimes Veerle asked: is she still breathing? And An said: it would be a nice death, slipping away with all those children round her.

I have resolved only to start crying when she is actually completely dead—that is, cold and no longer breathing. There is a bucket of amorphous pain inside me, into which I regularly tip all sorts of things before closing the lid again, and what eventually comes out of it and how, liquid or in splodges, we shall see. Give me the benefit of your understanding when it comes to the point. Today, I sat writing in the garden, which was exploding around me in growth—and me in the middle of it all, something like delicately blown glass on which the sun was breaking its milk teeth. The clouds were doing their best to look like Spanish armies, from the time of the Duke of Alva, with lances and halberds. The large specimens formed into citadels with steaming battlements to be captured—but there was one that couldn't be bothered and preferred to act in turn as a wheelbarrow, a tea cosy and a tricycle.

I had to persuade Dad that it has gradually become necessary to provide permanent residential care for my mother. He is aware of that, but finds it difficult to take in. He considers it betrayal, he feels guilty. So it was a cautious conversation. I with all my antennae alert steering a course round many cliffs so as not to offend him. He nodding, saying nothing, sobbing. But the conclusion was that shortly I shall be going to the nursing home with one of my sisters and putting Mum on the waiting list. So in a few months, given her condition, she will be leaving the house for good.

After the first shock he realizes that it is not the best but the least bad solution, and so do I. Nevertheless I am racked with guilt. I am pushing my mother out of the house, because there's no alternative. My father is crying with misery. Oh, I say nothing, I look out of the window at how beautifully blue the evening is. The white poplar waves a thousand grey-green crib sheets at once.

There has been so much death in the last few years. Every few months or so standing at the deathbed of someone close numbs the heart. I should get the ash washed out of my pores. I should like once again to be the creature with the thousand vibrating cilia that shimmers with a rapture approaching despair at each leaf that falls from a branch, each fall of light or the ecstatic proximity of a still-unknown body with the bronze boom of all the intertwined histories, all the fears and longings it harbours, and which I want to read like braille, until the ink splashes onto the page out of sheer abundance. Without it writing is harder.

Stupidity, selfishness and health, that's what you need to be happy. But if the first is lacking, all is lost (Flaubert).

Day in, day out she walks round the house. She doesn't sit still for more than ten minutes at a time. She opens drawers she has left untouched for months or years, and looks and looks. I find her in the kitchen trying to spoon gravy from a pan, while holding a glass under the tap. It is as if her body is making a last effort to keep a grip on things.

She strolls through my study, for half an hour she walks from the living room to the hall to the dining room with my dictionary in her hands. Then she puts it on the window sill, trying to place it exactly parallel with the edge, and leaves it there.

I had imagined their old age differently. In twenty years or so they would be old, the roles would be reversed and it'd be us who looked after them. But their old age is suddenly on the doorstep, and won't go away. I smell it in their clothes, they no longer bother to change their underwear every day, I fear—a helper will have to come in. How would he be able to cope otherwise? She traipses round after him all day long. Even on the toilet he is scarcely alone. She clings to him. Everywhere and at every moment that one word she has left, Dad, rings out—ever more hoarsely.

Is this life then? I wonder aloud at breakfast. Yes, this is life, says Lieven. And we haven't seen the end of it yet.

In the intervals between writing—I work from the morning until about four in the afternoon—I am gradually preparing for another farewell: from my grandmother, my mother's mother. Her shoulder is not healing, after that fall she had a few months back. Increasingly she develops a high temperature, has problems with all kinds of infections and, mainly, mentally she has virtually "gone". She seems to have no sense of place or time, and when I last saw her she called me "Jozef", the name of her brother who was killed in the war. She said nothing else, apart from the the mumbled rosaries she prays every waking hour. It would surprise me if she makes it to Easter.

If she dies, I shall have to support my father for a few days, as my mother won't be much help to him. She herself, to my relief, reacts calmly to developments. It will be a release, she said to me—strikingly lucidly and without faltering.

She died on Thursday morning at about ten o'clock, the grandmother. While I was on the train home the Monday before, I had a call from my father, who told me that she was failing fast. My sisters, my brothers and I stood watch by her bedside. I'm glad she remembered me, although she was too weak to talk—she spoke with her eyes and squeezed my hand.

The calm and serenity with which she awaited the end of her life are moving and in an odd way also consoling. The days I spent alternately working on the novel and with her, and while I was writing in the garden I felt strangely "embedded" in existence.

My mother is very upset, which for us in itself, strangely enough, is reassuring; although there are days when a real conversation is no longer possible, she is more "intact" than we might sometimes think.

The funeral, after six days of not really profound grief, was more full of poignant melancholy—one can hardly call eighty-nine a case of cot death. Only after the service, in the cemetery, when the coffin lay there so alone, sunk in the grave, in the pouring rain, did I break down for a moment.

Now she rests beside my grandfather, which is a consolation, near the avenue to the château. A very beautiful part of the village where I grew up—one of the landscapes that are very dear to Lieven and me.

After the funeral meal we toured the area a bit, the woods of Alter, and the old arable lands around the Bruges canal. The rain had washed away all the dust from the previous warm days, a bluish mist hung over the countryside and everything looked so green. Ancestral ground too, because at the foot of the embankment of the canal there is still the farm where my grandmother was born. After lying empty for years the house and the animal quarters are now being restored. It did me good to see it all again. In the last few years I have gone home frequently, but almost exclusively to provide sick-care, without taking much time for long walks or thinking things over.

Now we are left with boxes and cases and the always-too-scanty messages on posthumous paper.

It comes so easily to us, speaking and writing. One word brings the next with it, one silence splits like a shell around the next. If I am in the kitchen chopping vegetables, I think of her garbled language and wonder: what must it be like in that head of yours? Do all those cells sometimes accidentally intermesh again, and is self-consciousness suddenly created? Who am I and who are you? What do I still mean to you, and who are you to me? I can no longer remember when you were still well. That's why I hack away so recklessly at that leek.

At table, as she is drinking a glass of lemonade, it goes down the wrong way and she coughs.

I hear the timbre of her voice in her coughing.

I recognize her.

It gave me a fright, says Lieven afterwards. I suddenly heard Nelly again.

She hasn't said anything for months.

When we told him, when we had to tell him that his wife had Alzheimer's, he said: I want to look after her myself for as long as possible.

We'll sort that out, we said. And we also said it was better if she herself didn't know. Unless she gave very clear signs of an awareness that something was wrong with her.

Our doctor said: in my experience it's better not to give relatively young Alzheimer patients the diagnosis. It's highly likely they will develop a serious depression on top of their dementia. It's better if she can enjoy the lucid years she has left.

We shall have to face it, we said, and together try to make the best of it.

He was silent.

Later I rang him.

We've eaten and now we're watching TV, he said. Mum is lying on the sofa. She's had a bath and already has her night-dress on and she's nice and snug under a blanket on the sofa. Aren't you, Mum?

Only now do I realize: the days when I call him and she stands behind him prompting him what to say, what to ask, are over.

And only now do I remember that I called her one day and she said a letter had arrived for me, and that I asked her to open it and see what it was. And that she said, yes, I will, wait. And that she hung up and never rang back.

We thought: she won't get over it. In quick succession her father dead, her only sister dead. She herself has had cancer, fortunately detected in good time, and operations on her intestines and womb. She who prided herself on looking ten or fifteen years younger. She hadn't been herself for a while—what does that mean, not being yourself?

When we suggested she have an examination she thought the cancer had come back and that we knew and were keeping it from her. So when I said: you haven't got cancer, but you must realize you sometimes forget things, and that it wasn't that bad, that there were certain to be pills for it, she was so relieved that she never thought about anything else again.

I'm glad that she had another two or three years' carefree existence, although it leaves a bad taste to see someone disappearing into oblivion with an unsuspecting smile. We are the ones who are constantly saying goodbye to someone who is still there, and yet not.

The illness rages on. We have arranged for home care. The days of mental fog are beginning to gain the upper hand over the increasingly rare moments of relative lucidity. My father still wants to look after her himself. The disease is also wreaking havoc with her biorhythms, so that he sleeps with one eye open at night, which is untenable in the long term.

I can deal with it—or so I like to tell myself—while maintaining a warm-hearted distance, as it were. I have already said goodbye to her old self, to the woman I knew and who was my mother, once. Now I try to see her as a lively, sometimes restless, sometimes fearful child, who is playing in the recesses of a woman in her sixties and is growing back towards the very beginning.

How superficial life is. What more is a body than a handful of surfaces, piled in cavities, hung up from ribcages, bones? Iron out all those folds, lung tissue, intestinal tissue, all the convolutions of the brain, and you're not left with much more than so many square metres of self-aware slime, a wafer-thin membrane that breathes, digests, desires and thinks.

He calls. To say she's had a fall. She was walking behind him while he was vacuuming and tripped over the lead.

I think: why on earth are you still vacuuming, someone's coming in to help, aren't they? But I ask: did she hurt herself?

A nasty gash in her forehead, which needed stitches. Now she's all black and blue, and she's crying.

She's been crying for a few days. When she gets up, at breakfast, when the nurse comes to wash her hair, she is quiet. Once she's dressed it starts up. She squeaks, a soft moaning. It never stops. She comes in whining, gets up from table whining and leaves again whining on my father's arm. She whines while she drinks lemonade. Still whining, she pushes the biscuit into her mouth.

How long will the place here in the house mean biscuit to her? It has long since ceased to mean her son, or the cats or Lieven.

She whines because she is afraid she'll have to go back in the car (in the car she's quiet, says my father), and because she'll again be dragged from pillar to post all day long, out of the car, into the house, into the car, because he can't stand being alone with her and her decay (and you can't ask him to stay at home the whole time).

She whines with misery, with fear, with grief. With the rage that she takes out on his upper arm with her impotent blows. She whines because she'd like to be quiet somewhere, but that somewhere doesn't exist.

I'd rather not imagine, but I do anyway: her walking doglike after him, the only person she still recognizes and on whom she fixates like a dove on the dovecote. Him first putting her on the sofa, picking up the vacuum cleaner again, but then giving up after she comes trailing after him for the umpteenth time.

The macabre dance of the two of them behind the vacuum cleaner round the table, she getting her feet caught in the cable and falling to the floor. Her crying. The blood. His feeling of guilt. The doctor.

I call back and ask: how can you stand it, I'm all in after a quarter of an hour.

He says: It's not that bad, I can take it.

Was that absent-mindedness of hers always a portent? How many times did she sprinkle sugar instead of salt on the beef-steak and fail to understand why the gravy turned to caramel? Afternoons when the smell of burnt potatoes wafted towards us as soon as we reached the garden gate—countless. The house was an ordeal for indoor plants: languishing leaves over dried-out clods of compost—while the cactus drowned. In her hands the wash was a bureaucratic nightmare. Shirts, missing for weeks, suddenly turned up again—or disappeared without trace.

What else has she covered up? Was it always there? Are the meshes in her brain now becoming fatally wide? Was it written in her nerve cells, from the beginning?

Christmas Eve, the first Christmas since it became visible. Tarrying in the kitchen, to give the impression that she is lending a hand; her fingers with the knife in them linger above the onion and the chopping board. She studies the onion, the knife and the chopping board. Finally she puts the knife down, takes a tea towel and rubs the work surface clean with it for the umpteenth time, then the edge of the kitchen unit.

We say nothing, ignore it, and roll our eyes. Wondering: does she know? Is she keeping up appearances for herself?

Or did it begin (when do these things begin?) when we noticed that she was mesmerized by the toddlers' programme on television? With childlike fascination she watched the puppets sliding across the screen, the colourful, constantly changing chequerboard patterns, the dancing, opening and closing parasols.

I like that, she said, these days.

They were going to visit friends. She stands in front of the bathroom mirror flabbergasted: a white mask stares out at her with her own terrified eyes. She tries to wipe it off but simply rubs the white further over her cheeks, her forehead and her nose. She looks at her fingers, at the tube, at her fingers again. She comes into the kitchen like that.

This is funny face cream I bought, she says.

Mum, says one of my sisters, that's toothpaste.

———

If a word does not come immediately to mind, I think: it's started. If I find the salt cellar in the fridge after hunting for several minutes, I panic. This afternoon I was having a pee and I saw that I had put my pen in the mug on the shelf over the washbasin, with the toothbrushes.

They have one last trip together, with a couple they know, to Asia to visit her oldest brother. The doctors think she can manage that.

In their absence my sisters find the house in a state of disorder. Old washing stuffed into the unused washing machine. Secreted washing-up full of dry crusts, waiting for soap and suds.

How long has he been hiding all kinds of things from us?

Meanwhile, on the other side of the world she is shocking the company with attacks of rage, fear and complete derangement. In the plane she won't sit still. She scolds her best friend, thinking that she fancies my father.

Everything is crumbling.

On the beach, as she watches the bronzed, horny young people on the silver sand under the palms, she makes as if to lift her skirt and cries out despairingly: look, I can't do it any more. I can't do it any more.

Later in the photos I see that she's gone. Fog in her eyes. A look I don't recognize. What's become of her?

In the following months it goes from bad to worse. The blonde with which she colours her hair grows out, making way for grey. She loses weight visibly. In the winter months she literally shakes with cold. Overnight she is a woman in her late eighties.

At each new collapse we swallow, and make the best of it.

Sometimes we wonder: us too? Soon? When?

It goes like a flash, decay. If we had imagined a slow decline, at a pace that would be more or less bearable for my father, as far as that is possible, we can lay that dream to rest. In the space of a few weeks the remnants of self-awareness or consciousness that were in her have vanished. It is as if you're looking from the top of a cliff at a huge whirlpool, as if I am embracing an hourglass of skin and bone. The erosion is unstoppable and horrifying.

The panic in her eyes, it is as if she is watching the house around her being emptied by a gang of looters, too perplexed and powerless to stop them. Hands grabbing everywhere. We've scarcely turned our backs, so to speak, before the thieves have made off with yet another word or a habit.

Sometimes she sits shaking on the sofa, I don't know if it's from fear or grief, or is she cold because her internal thermostat has gone haywire?

I look at her, she looks back, with a helplessness that cuts you to the quick. I hear the rustling of the rats behind the panelling, gnawing at her nerves.

A friend whose mother also had Alzheimer's once said: it's the most cowardly, sneakiest disease I know. It wrung my mother out like a floorcloth and slung her in a corner.

I can hear it giggling, the disease, behind the cupboard, under the table, in a cowardly tone.

Another friend told me about a woman who kept going at home by sticking self-adhesive labels everywhere, on the doors, on cupboards and other furniture, with words like "soup plates", "cups" or "beer glasses" on them.

I wondered: does she stick a label on her blouse too, with "Me" on it in mirror writing, so that she knows who it is who bends over the washbasin in the mornings to freshen her face? And how long will it be before she no longer knows what reading is—like my mother; panicking in a whirlpool of labels that have come loose?

She plants her nails in the flesh of my forearm until it almost bleeds when we take her out for a walk with us, and if she could she would huddle up in me while she stares in fearful incomprehension at the fields that have surrounded her since her earliest childhood.

In the mornings the restlessness strikes as soon my father has served her breakfast. He puts her in the car and drives off with her. Fleeing from emptiness at home, he tries to find warmth with us and especially with my sisters, which is not always convenient—but we drop what we are doing, if only for fifteen minutes or half an hour. We make coffee, give him a chance to calm down, although we know that shortly, at about four-thirty, she'll want to be off again, and by about seven-thirty she'll be in bed and the only sound that rings out will be that of the television.

You can't say anything any more, nothing, he sighs. She doesn't respond to anything. Nothing at all comes back.

The great sower of feelings of guilt is bringing in its rich harvest. We, feeling guilty because we can't be there more often than we already are. He, feeling guilty when he has to give up any aspect of caring for her. Arranging for home care, bringing in a home help, and each time having the feeling you're betraying him because he has the feeling he's betraying her. We must try to get through this—I can't imagine the havoc a disease like this must wreak in a family where they've never really got on, where all the dormant conflicts are exposed, in all their rawness.

At night she pulls up her legs in her sleep and then stretches them again. It drives him crazy.

Perhaps you shouldn't sleep together any more, I say.

He shrugs his shoulders: I've tried the sofa in the living room a few times.

After a week or so that habit subsides, but her sleep becomes longer and deeper.

When will she not wake up again?

Sometimes I catch myself looking around me and wondering about those in my immediate circle: if you were to die, how great would the pain be? As if something like that can be assessed. Still, I try, as it were, to measure the depth of the knife wounds and tend to weigh the value of friendships and affections against a non-existent loss. Sometimes I sit reading on the sofa and see Lieven's face on the cushion beside me—and I have to fight back the tears. Sometimes I'm with friends and I think: don't go yet, don't fall apart too soon.

Is that how it will be from now on? Is that the hush of older relations, as I remember them from parties in the past, when I found them nothing but a heap of gout and crutches in the shadow of the pines, surveying the youngsters around them, drinking, cooing and filled with reflection? I mean the awareness that behind your back the chilly wall of the eternal ice age is sliding closer, pushing mountains of rubble ahead of it, and that nothing can be done about it.

Mourning: someone throws a clammy floorcloth over the sun. Someone draws tiny lines in your chest with a razor blade. And on a godforsaken street corner, for the first time in years, you bump into your own pale self. The shadow leers: reunited at last.

She has become a mirror. If we look cheerful, she is too—more or less. If the worries and grief are written on our faces, she too is overcome by sadness. But recently, recently she is increasingly stuck in what seems to be a permanent state of disruption. I can only hope that there is very little awareness of time left, that there is no sense in her that it used to be different, better. That thought is never able to console for long. Having to live in an eternal now of fear is perhaps just as great a torture—nothing but present, nothing but panic.

Sometimes, when she fixes me with her look, I think that some mechanism in her brain scans for all signs of emotion, in my face, in my whole body. If I act more cheerful than I feel, I can't calm her down. Somewhere in her brain, some circuit or other picks up the fact that I am behaving differently than my mood dictates. Perhaps an instinct that is more or less intact and possibly comes more to the fore now that the complex functions of thinking and speaking have virtually collapsed.

Whenever I wake her, he says, when I wake her, because I have to wake her, otherwise she may go on sleeping, she always laughs, happy as a child.

Surely it must be, he says, that she still remembers me?

She's in hospital. While they were having breakfast, my father noticed that she suddenly went as white as a sheet. Her eyes rolled, her arms and legs started jerking. He lifted her up, her bony body that had become as light as a feather, laid her on the sofa and called the doctor. He rang us, but kept getting the voicemail. When I listened to the message I heard the panic in his voice: Mum's had a kind of turn.

I rang him at once, and he had already calmed down somewhat, but his voice broke when he said: I thought I'd lost her.

So straight onto the train, to the most depressing provincial town imaginable, and the weather isn't particularly helpful today. The doctors haven't found anything, it may be connected with the medication, the mild sedative that she has to take in the evening, to which she is reacting badly. Very probably they will adjust the dose or try something else. It's not exactly cheerful having to spend a day in a geriatric unit and I'd rather not imagine what it's like to spend your last few days there. Whenever I have to go there I am overcome with rage and terror. This is the hidden monoculture of our welfare state, I think. Fields and fields of grizzled heads, sagging, half-depressed (lonely, probably) or anxious (also lonely, perhaps), and crammed with pills for want of human companionship. I think I'd rather string myself up if it ever gets to this point. As a neighbour of ours in this street did a few years ago, next door, on the landing from one of the rails of the banisters.

I'm almost certain that our grandmother, when she was forced to go into a home after that heavy fall on her bike, reached the conclusion privately that enough was enough. When she arrived and saw the building, which looks like a hospital, which smells like a hospital, which constantly screams in your face from the neon light fittings on the ceiling and the white material worn by the nursing staff that old age is a disease—she probably decided: that's enough for me.

I'd bet my boots that when, in addition to the fractures she had sustained, she caught some mysterious intestinal infection, she gave nature a helping hand and said to her God, for whom in those last few months she said the rosary day in, day out: my husband dead. My oldest daughter dead. And now watching another of my children die. Out of the question. It's my turn now. After which she started eating less and less.

I fumed, not to say boiled with rage at the crassness of that nurse who, with her hand in that of a fully conscious dying woman, was moved to say: it won't be much longer. When I did her toilet this morning there was already post-mortem lividity on her back.

She died on the morning of Ascension Day. Beyond the open window the church tower shook out sackfuls of carillon music over the roofs and the zenith was brilliant blue. In my life the nineteenth century was over. She died a death from another age, surrounded by the few saints' statues she had brought from home.

And here I sit as I write this, in a corner of the hospital corridor, in which my mother is washed and is terrified: plastic everywhere, down to the indoor plants, above my head a neurotic neon tube.

It happened again, while she was sleeping on the sofa in the afternoon. My father had gone to see family and I had promised to "mummy-sit". She went pale in her sleep, her cheeks almost as white as this paper. Under her eyelids I saw the pupils gliding towards the top edge of her eye sockets and from her trunk and midriff a series of shocks passed through her limbs. I slid one hand under her neck, and laid the other on her belly, and meanwhile I kept my eyes on her face and her lips, to see whether there were any convulsions with which she could have hurt her tongue, but I saw that under the thin skin of her mouth she was simply biting down hard on her teeth.

It lasted for a minute at most. I was worried sick, but at the same time I contemplated her and thought: go now, go on. If this is to be the moment, go then, let go, it doesn't matter. But the convulsions ebbed away, and she came round and looked at me and smiled. My eyes filled with tears, to tell the truth, and I felt, as it were, my whole life, my whole idiotic, humdrum life, from the sandpit to the wheelchair in which I shall doubtless end up cursing or gaga, trembling in me.

Should I get dementia, it will be evident from my handwriting. It will become more legible, for other eyes too. Years of writing at night and in the quiet hours have distorted my private handwriting till it has become a sort of intimate stenography—a series of dots and curls and other score marks which have become a highly personal memory aid for me. If I, as we say in these parts, start misfiring, my writing will undoubtedly become slower, and automatically neater—if there is anything left to write about.

Even now it regularly happens that I need half an hour to decipher passages that I have written the night before in handwriting that hobbles along in clogs after the ecstasy of inspiration. And yet it doesn't annoy me. Indeed, I find it reassuring to be able to sit and stare at my notes as if they were a millennia-old clay tablet, which may preserve a forgotten epic or the inventory of the temple storerooms round the altar of the earth goddess.

She always said that my handwriting was like her sister's: just as illegible or anyway difficult to decipher. Her own handwriting bore the mark of school all her life, rather more angular than the calligraphy she had been taught in the 1950s. Letters to the head teacher, when we were ill or absent for some other reason, invariably contained references to "my son" or "my daughter", which surprised us.

She never talked about us like that.

I would like to read the letters, the masses of letters she wrote to her sister the nun, usually sitting on the edge of her bed.

She wrote with a blue biro on squared paper.

Her signature was easy to forge. We all regularly signed school reports and suchlike—to which she more or less turned a blind eye. She was not very keen on the growing paper mountain generated by an education system obsessed with forms.

She wrote to her sister often when her sister got cancer. I should like to know how her consolation sounded, her concern, perhaps her own fear too.

Every day I repeat the miracle—or better the triumph—of the moment when our species invented writing. Reading and writing are things that we eventually do without thinking. Again and again the nimble-fingered miracle of our memory that, word by word, syllable by syllable, recalls the totally arbitrary link between a letter and a sound and what that association means. Again and again the creation of meaning from a dreadful background interference which without the other person's ear would not convey any message... And that miracle, that everyday explosion into meaning, crackles and sparks back in time, to the ports of the Phoenicians, to the kings of Sumer, to the glazed tiles of the tower of Babel, scattered in the sand.

Shortly after she became ill, when she was here in my house and could not think of the word "book", my father showed her a newspaper report, something about a book of mine that was about to come out. It took her a quarter of an hour to read the article. And when I asked her if she understood what was in it, she nodded, but I could tell she was lying from the uncertain way she looked at my father.

Hickory. Dickory. Dock. The words are deserting her again. She is de-wording and de-languaging and de-remembering.

We learned to read through books about a boy and girl called Jan and Fien. They had a dog called Pim. I can remember being moved and astonished when they introduced me to the word "home". The fact that, by replacing two letters with one the magic constitution of the word "house" changed, I found miraculous.

So I learn to read and write anew every day—this miracle moves me every day afresh, more strongly, more intensely than before. Our home no longer exists, but I distribute, as it were, the family affection we knew, which was given to us, my brothers and sisters and me, in generous helpings, over a dozen braziers to store it elsewhere. You. Sweet. Warm. Kiss.

Present for Mother's Day?
Buy her a good book!

Read our checklist of the best gift books!

Top sellers for Mother's Day,
sure to please!

She gets up from the table, goes to the kitchen. When she comes back into the room she catches sight of herself in the big mirror against the wall next to the table. For minutes on end she tries to avoid her own reflection, in order to sit with that of my father and me at the reflected table. She is like the robin that pecks at its own reflection in the window pane. She no longer knows that the woman whose face is contorted with pain and fear is herself.

When she comes to us, I have to close the curtain quickly, says Veerle. Otherwise she walks from the hall slap bang into the French windows.

Where does that behaviour come from that she sometimes exhibits? That wells up out of her and ebbs away again? Why does she suddenly start taking her skirt in one hand when she gets up from the sofa, so that in a caricature of coquettishness she wobbles through the living room with one bare knee?

It disappears, after a while. But then she is suddenly fixated on shoes. She takes a pair of slippers from under the radiator in the kitchen and goes upstairs with them (with me behind her, terrified she will fall), and traipses round from room to room with them, crying. Until I sit down and she flops down on the sofa beside me half an hour later and allows me to stroke her back, too exhausted to ward me off.

I imagine I can hear it, the silent havoc spreading through that body: strings that break, wires that snap, high-tension cable singing as it gives out—the soft moan of collapsing beams. My mother, a house that is slowly collapsing, a bridge dancing to a tremor. Sometimes she falls asleep even before her shoulders reach the back of the sofa. She remains hanging there asleep, hands in front of her. Short spasms run continually through her wrists and fingers. The last pylons are still standing, but they are rocking.

We're terrified. We don't say much about it, but we're terrified. Terrified of what is to come, however inevitable it may be. Terrified of mourning, which we would like to start today, in order not to have to stay in this twilight zone between life and death. It is neither fish nor fowl, day nor night, death nor life. The disease is kicking her out of time and booting us out of language. Words seem to me a kind of breakfast cereal at the moment: undoubtedly healthy, but rather tasteless.

Another Christmas Eve, with and without her. Another Christmas Eve, with grandchildren who can't understand why their granny is so sad and acts so strangely. I bend down to her, in her wheelchair, where she is sitting calmly, with a glass of alcohol-free bubbly in her hand and a bowl of nibbles. The edge of the table must more or less mark the boundary between the space, the narrow space around her, where the world is still familiar and reassuring, and the world outside, which confuses her and frightens her.

We do our best to have her at table with us, but the outside world that frightens her, us that is, is obviously coming too close. She wants to get up and walk away.

We roll her back to her corner of the room, some distance away, where she calms down. At ten o'clock Father takes her to bed.

We say nothing about it for the rest of the evening, but everyone thinks what I'm thinking: for the first time in thirty or forty years midnight strikes and Christmas arrives without her being there.

I don't want to see her wasting away (and somehow I do, somehow I want to confront the proof of her disappearance). I don't want to see her all skin and bone twitching and trembling in her final bed (and I do want to see it), I don't want to have to think: this body that is shot through with attacks and spasms is no longer my mother (I'm prepared to think it if I have to). And I don't want to have to think too often: this trembling skeleton, this wreck, is still my mother (and I'm prepared to do that too). Why can't I say: she's no longer with us, without feeling a stab of pain in my ribcage? Why can't I say either: there is still something of her in her, without feeling pain too? And apart from that, if we decide that it's worthwhile to go on treating her for all kinds of things, for whom is it worthwhile? And if we were to decide that it's gradually become enough, for whom are we deciding that: for her or for us?

There are moments when I just chatter and chatter and chatter. I've never been a babbler and will never be one, and yet on some days I just chatter and chatter and chatter.

I chatter till I burst, chatter till I'm blue in the face and interrupt other people. I just rattle and gabble on, spew out language, teeth chattering, with a mouth full of dry oats. Where can I come ashore? And if I'm not chattering, I'm crying.

Last week my brothers-in-law brought our parents' bed downstairs. It seems trivial, but it's another of those apparently insignificant steps that mean the umpteenth concession to the disease. It will do him good, he'll no longer have to sleep with one eye open and jump up the moment she wakes in the middle of the night and stumbles towards the landing.

And yet everything is now empty upstairs. The house is growing prematurely old, like her.

Together at the window again, the two of us. He has popped out to the baker's, the post office or the chemist's.

Where is he, where is he now, you know, him, him, him…

Dad.

Yes, Dad.

Where is he, has he gone, where's he got to?

She's crying.

You mustn't be afraid. He'll be right back. Don't be afraid.

With her fingertips she fiddles with the hem of my shirt.

I'mafraidI'mafraid, she whispers.

At the same time I hear something dripping.

Between her feet the carpet darkens with her pee.

She hasn't noticed a thing.

I bend down, dry the carpet with a cloth, and wonder:

Does he always carry extra panties with him?

Did he also bend down, forty years ago, when her waters broke?

She didn't like babies, she liked being pregnant. One evening, when she was heavily pregnant with my youngest brother, she pulled her blouse up and stood in the light of the reading lamp looking at her belly. It seemed as big as the moon, that belly of hers, and she embraced it with both hands, blissfully. I never saw her cherish anything or anyone like that belly. Cherishing was something my father did, the man whom she bore children.

The whole family had gone to the Ardennes for the weekend (all my brothers and sisters and other halves and children, nineteen of us in all). A few days constantly around her showed us how far the illness has already progressed.

When we left on Sunday and wanted to say our goodbyes, she walked past me in order to take a red child's bike that was lying on the lawn to the shed. Leave her, said Lieven. But as I saw her disappearing across the lawn holding that bike a chasm of unattainability opened up. I was shattered by her isolation, because she herself is not aware of it.

It's good he's there, slightly at a distance from the emotions that the illness evokes in my father, and in my brothers and sisters and me.

That he's there, as it were on the bank, while we navigate a course round the cliffs in open water.

That he's there to make soup for, mash potatoes. Things become very concrete, like for example chopping a chicken into pieces to make a meal for us.

Having a good cry now and then is also part of it, of course, but also immersing myself in the day's routine. The fact that he has to get up for work, that he's ravenous when he gets home.

We've known each other since we were children, basically, and so as old fogeys we'd better make the best of it.

Sometimes I worry about later. Who will go first, who will have to bear the dull misery of being left behind? And the raging fear.

He will tough it out, I think. Draw in his neck, head thrust forward, and charge on. He is more inured to the hard aspects of life because life has been a lot tougher for him. I, I'm a pampered thoroughbred in that respect. I haven't been through anything.

There's no point in going on about it.

I'm going to make courgette soup tonight, with a handful of coriander.

He likes strong flavours.

I'd so like to have a cheerfully demented mother. One of those good-humoured, ever-upbeat ladies who still go to the hairdresser's, albeit at three in the morning. One of those cackling aunties or out-of-control grannies who wet themselves laughing and miss the cup when pouring tea—our Hollywood dementia patients.

I can't stand them, the colour-photogenic senile models, the pin-ups of those countless books which prattle on with such insufferable exuberance about Alzheimer's also creating opportunities. Give me anything, if necessary a moaning harpy, a Bacchanal of ungovernable surliness or lewd talk. Not this wreck of a woman, so lean and emaciated by now that it strikes me how wide the crown of her head is, making me wonder: was she brought into the world with forceps sixty-five years ago?

She now walks to and fro round the house, all day long. She gets up off the sofa, goes to the kitchen, from the kitchen to the bathroom, from the bathroom back to the kitchen and from the kitchen to the hall and back again. I can count myself lucky that she no longer wants to go upstairs with a pair of shoes in her hands to put them away in a last paroxysm of domesticity in a wardrobe that has long since been dismantled.

The house smells of dust and emptiness upstairs—downstairs, all day long, the shuffling of soles across the floor and that human frame, clothes, skin and steel wire, from the front door to the back door, the arms lame alongside the body like a stray puppet in a clock mechanism.

Constantly sitting, crying, getting up, searching, sitting, crying and getting up again. No touch brings any rest; no song can calm her down. Only "Mum, for Christ's sake sit down" helps—sometimes.

Gradually I begin to understand the euphemism lurking beneath the charming designation "home care". Looking after sick family members yourself, with the support of district nurses—it sounds good.

Home care, as if we were still living in the late nineteenth century, when families averaged twelve hundred children apiece and there was an extensive network of cousins, aunts, uncles and relations more or less under one roof.

The district nurse is on sick leave, drained and burnt out and out of circulation for about three months. The home help who comes to clean has to recover every so often from her hectic daily round up hill and down dale to the umpteenth farm where an elderly farmer or farmer's wife sits by the stove waiting for help.

In the paper I read that in England home care produces a saving for the NHS larger than the total education budget.

In our hospitals the vertebrae of nursing staff who twist their backs lifting the products of the ageing society are grinding.

Who wipes his arse with whom here?

Arise you workers from your slumbers, etc.

She said I can always ring her, the nurse, says my father. Even though she's on sick leave.

You can call me, she said. Any time. Just you.

He needs to go into hospital for a minor procedure, nothing serious, but she has to be admitted too, there's no alternative. The surgeon has arranged for a room for her in the secure geriatric unit.

I go with them. Two cases, one for him, one for her.

She is restless. She seems to realize that something is up, that she will be separated from my father, if only for about three nights.

She still always feels for my hand when I come to bed, he says.

Forms.

We must regard your mother's stay as an ordinary admission.
So we must fill out an admission form, says the duty neurologist.

Can your mother still wash by herself?

No, she can't.

Eat and drink?

No, she can't do that either.

Can your mother still get dressed and undressed?

I shake my head.

Is the home adapted for persons with a handicap?

They've been sleeping and living downstairs for months, I say.
But I'm thinking: stop it, woman.

―――――――

The next day we find her slumped in the chair by the window, with her chin against the edge of the table that has been clamped onto the arms of the chair. She is crying and frightened to death. Her hands are grabbing in all directions. Her soles are sliding across the floor as they've forgotten to lower the footrest. We help her up, and in the skin of her lower jaw is the blood-red imprint of the edge of the table.

She is silent and I am silent too. She with a head full of holes, I with a mouth full of plaster. Outside drizzle, the grey backs of buildings, wind in folded parasols. In the corridor the jolting of trolleys and the clatter of plates. At the nursing station a telephone bleeps. No one picks up. The nurse says: fortunately she ate well.

———

She goes from room to room, up and down the length of the corridor, the side corridor, the stairwell, as far as the glass door with the combination lock and the lift. She wants to go in everywhere, except into her own room. Then fear takes hold, she starts to cry and I can feel her muscles stiffening.

After the umpteenth attempt I lift her up and am hit in the process, put her in the chair by the window and clamp the table onto the armrests. Then I take her hand in mind and hum songs—for one, two hours. Children's songs, folk songs, what I can still remember of the Gregorian repertoire.

She calms down. With her free hand she taps on the back of mine, then on the table top. She puts her thumb and forefinger together and seems to want to write something. Then she looks at me. Some more tears. We hum "Veni Creator Spiritus".

When she calms down, sleep comes. One hand hangs in the air above the table top. Behind her glasses the eyelids fall shut, although they never seem to close completely. The eyelashes go on trembling, as if as soon as the eyes close the dreaming phase begins. The muscles in her neck relax, her head falls forward.

That's how she sleeps, one hand hangs in the air for a while, and then sinks down next to the other. Sometimes her breathing becomes more regular, deeper, and a slow tidal movement ebbs and flows through her bones. Her sleeping skull rocks above the table—how thin she is.

For the fifth or sixth time she walks round the entire physio-therapy room with me, at the end of the corridor. Again she feels her way along the edge of the basket with the bunch of dried flowers, again she tries to pop the colourful pebbles in the bowl next to the bunch of dried flowers into her mouth and I extract them laboriously from between her smacking lips. And again, for the umpteenth time, she takes from a cabinet the little metal churn which, with all the rest of the kitsch, attempts in vain to brighten up the clinical area, and takes it to the kitchen corner and the draining board. Halfway she stops, uncertain, and then with the churn in her hand walks from one side of the room to the other, sobbing.

When, for the umpteenth time in a row, I sit down on one of the chairs round the kitchen table and say: I don't know what you want, Mum, but I'm going to rest a bit, she simply comes and tugs at my shoulders and gives me weak slaps because I won't budge.

Meanwhile Mrs B. comes in, and stands by another table in the room, in shiny pyjamas and holding a good-sized wallet.

Well I never, she says. Old acquaintances!

My mother whines.

Do we know each other then? Where do you live?

In Grammene, replies Mrs B.

That's possible. Relations of ours used to live there.

So you don't know who I am?

No.

So what am I doing standing here?

I wouldn't know.

Neither would I, says Mrs B.

A little later her therapist arrives. Mrs B. reads the paper aloud, the paper of her area. Pigeon-racing. Cycling news. Accident with minor damage and four injured.

What have you just read? Tell me, asks the therapist.

Who has read what? asks Mrs B. in astonishment.

———

The nurse brings her coffee. Smacking her lips, she looks at the cup that is put on the window sill. Give it to me, give it to me, her hands gesture. The corners of her mouth tremble, as if a last remnant of articulation still animates her lips.

She drinks greedily and polishes off the biscuit. When the cup is empty and the biscuit finished, she remains restless. She points to the silvery plastic the biscuit came in. All afternoon she makes it crackle in her fingertips and watches mesmerized, puts it in her mouth, sucks on it, crumples it in her fingers and sucks again.

She looks at me: don't take it away from me.

Finally she falls asleep again and I leave her alone. In the doorway I turn round. I see her figure, hunched in sleep, hanging over the table, her arms pulled into her body, neck pulled into her shoulders, head bent forward, fingers curled on her ribcage. Her body is taking over from her, is lowering the blinds over her battered brain and is automatically filling her lungs. She rocks in her sleep. I think: so this is my mother.

I take the stairs down, behind the combination lock ("please key in the date backwards and push the gate"). The doors of most rooms are open, behind them grey hair, sucking on lower lips. Smell of ether, and the whole muzak of a hospital corridor on an endless grey afternoon. Games with bells ringing, telebingo, buzzing telephones, snatches of Brazilian soaps. This is where they rest then, the worker bees now shrunk to larvae of the welfare state, which is bursting at the seams under their weight…

Downstairs the nurse says my father is already out of recovery but that he's in a different room. The man he was sharing the room with died this afternoon and is now being laid out.

It doesn't surprise me. This morning, in the bed next to my father's, I saw a trunk without legs, groaning in its sleep and with the death rattle already audible in its windpipe.

He's dead, that guy, says my father.

Yes, I say.

Apart from that he is silent, still slightly woozy from the anaesthetic.

When my sisters visit towards evening, they haven't got my message.

Have you come for the gentleman? asks the perplexed nurse. Didn't they call you? The gentleman died...

What? Dead? Mr Mortier. My father? cries Veerle.

No, the other gentleman, replies the nurse, relieved.

I thought, that's it, says Veerle later. We'll have to cope all by ourselves.

She falls, for the umpteenth time. In my father's room, where after the nurse has brought the evening meal, she panics. She gets up. I see her wobble. Shout something because I am standing too far away from her. My brothers are also too late. She goes straight forward on her face. The reflex of spreading her hands in front of her and breaking her fall with her arms has long since disappeared.

The thud of her head on the floor. The desperation. The frame of her glasses has dug into her eyebrow. She wails tears and blood.

To Accident and Emergency. The wound must be stitched. Again. I say: we can easily look for different frames for her. My brothers and sister take her away. One pushes the wheelchair, the others take her hands in theirs. Pietà. The sons carry the mother.

The sitting,
That sitting of hers,

next to me on the sofa.

That sitting without anything,
and that silence: an empty
house in the afternoon,

the tap leaks.

During the dinner for my father's birthday, in that restaurant in the fields, she beckoned me from the wheelchair in which she almost always sits now. She beckoned me as she used to at family parties or other occasions where it was hectic: with her forefinger crooked and the hint of a wink.

I got up almost by reflex from my chair and went over to her, at the other end of the table. She smiled faintly and I smiled back. It can only have been about three steps, but as I walked towards her I saw the clarity disappear from her eyes and the mist rose again. Whatever it had been, it had gone.

It's hard to adjust to life and, hardest of all, to death.

What I can't cope with is her complete helplessness. The unbearable thought that if there were no one else there, she might survive for only a day or two. She would still have the reflex to drink when she's thirsty, and for all we know, if they were within reach, she might be able to bring a spoon or a glass to her mouth. But actions like turning on a tap she has long since forgotten. She would not be able to dress or wash herself, or change her underwear; she would be helplessly lost.

Sometimes I observe her, I see her walking past the kitchen window, back and forth, woodenly, with her hands in front of her, to and fro, to and fro like a pendulum—the loneliness is almost audible, the eternal whistling of a kettle just below boiling point.

We live in and outside time. The seasons go on succeeding each other, but the usual time seems just a skin at present, surrounding dark, timeless flesh, of which she forms the bitter kernel. I wish time would revolve again. We have become crepuscular beings, searching and groping in twilight, unsure whether it will ever become day or night.

Sometimes she stops the pendulum movement for a moment. She looks at me as if I am something that has occurred to her.

And then goes on walking.

She is a girl with a bag of marbles that splits open, and she looks in terror as they career across the floor.

She has opened a cupboard and all the crockery tumbles out over her, there's no end to it.

She has lost her way in a labyrinth of drying sheets.

She is stuck in the mud and tries in vain to pull one leg loose.

She puts a lump of sugar in her mouth and her whole being, or what is left of it, sucks on it for all it is worth and everything in her relaxes, as if her organism remembers what sweetness is—as if her organism is relieved that it remembers sweetness.

She pulls on the hem of the undercloth on the table. She tries to lay the hem parallel to the edge of the table, again and again.

She cries and she laughs and she cries and she laughs, four or five times a minute.

My mother,
for a whole morning she searches for a word
as a cornerstone to fill the breach.

For a whole morning the bitten hole
of that word stands missing between us.

Mother's word for today is erosion.

She stammers alluvially: the lilacs are still what's
that called when they have no leaves—bare.

Whether there will be ice on the pond is uncertain this year,
whether it will be strong enough to—
her fingers skate.

She says days are wintry
and they are.

She also says: what are those clicks, no
Clocks, you know, in the grass,
On legs, they're laying but that one isn't.

He's just crowing. So funny
those things there
in the grass with cats.

Is it so windy today,
or are those my thoughts?

Will a day come when no one
remembers the right mistakes, no one still
knows what speech impediment

exactly to feed?

Will anyone bore through your sandcastles
of semantics with
firebreaks and understanding?

Why, after each mouthful, does she always
wipe the rim of the cup dry with her thumb?

Why do simple sweet wrappers suddenly become
transparent mysteries?

Why do I see her testing with her lips, the tip
of her tongue the difficult corners

of words as if she is
standing on a narrow ledge with her back

against the wall—why doesn't she dare
to look down, and does she say

that something's dizzy there?

—————

Back home our mother goes visibly downhill. My father cannot see the reality and is balancing on the edge of a depression (for which there must be pills, but what good are they?). It threatens to infect us all. Inwardly I sometimes have the feeling that I am slowly transforming into some dull, colourless metal, with very little resonance. Something like zinc or tin: as solid as it is grey.

She collapsed. Her muscle tone is weakening. She can scarcely move her fingers or toes any longer. Slowly she is curling into the foetal position. It may be connected with the cold, with this long winter. Perhaps it will soon improve.

My father clings to any sign that somewhere in that languishing organism the woman he knows still lives. Some while ago I met my brothers and sisters to open up and get drunk—but also to establish whether we all agreed that a point is coming at which we will have to decide to put an end to the suffering. It sounds businesslike, but when the moment comes it will nevertheless be a dreadful decision—or, who knows, who knows, a release.

We have decided against a thorough periodic examination. The GP will keep an eye on her condition and if there are complications she can always go to the hospital.

What is the point of shoving her under a scanner every three or four months?

Subjecting her to the horror of a spinal puncture to find out what we actually already know—that the substances that are making her ill are not going away, on the contrary—would simply be a token of sadism.

Nor will she be given any pills which supposedly slow the degeneration of her nervous system, because the pills don't do that. They are magic balls, that's all, like extensive swathes of medical jargon: magic formulae with an ancient etymology that hangs our mother out to dry between the pages of a textbook.

For us doctors are not healers but interpreters: what we know in ordinary words they translate into terms of Greek and Latin origin. Leave philology out of it. I like doctors who don't know everything either and say that in so many words. They exist, but they're becoming rare.

I don't want her to fall into the hands of some white-coated type who double-checks everything against his protocol of statistically backed bullet points and has scarcely any ear or eye for the person she still is.

Look and listen, listen closely, says our GP. And talk, but that is difficult with your mum, of course.

Mum, I remember, one of the first winters where it was clear to everyone how ill you were, sitting here on the chair by the window, and it was cold outside, bitterly cold. You were sitting right next to the radiator, the faintly ticking radiator. If you'd been able to, you would have crawled inside it. You held your hands against the warm side, all your fingers spread wide, and shivered and shivered.

I don't know if you remember—no, you can't possibly remember, I forget how old I was, perhaps about ten. We went to visit Lea in Ghent. We were walking along the Lousbergskaai; you were carrying my younger brother on your arm and at a street corner your foot slipped off the edge of the kerb and you fell.

My brother finished up on the asphalt, bawling. I remember I picked him up. You crawled to your feet—grazed knees, torn tights. You swore and bit back your tears, and pulled the tails of your jacket straight, that rust-coloured check two-piece, over your fake crocodile leather shoes. I remember thinking, or rather it being whispered from my gut: mothers die too.

Why do we accept the mortality of our fathers more easily than that of our mothers? Because the tough thread of life is spun from mothers? I think of your fingers on that radiator: so fragile, almost translucent, like the newly opened fingers of a foetus, through which the first blood vessels meander their way.

You fell, two summers ago, during the very last walk we all went on together. The Ardennes, end of September: the earth a carpet of dry leaves and husks, the smell of dew and vegetable decay. Somewhere on the descent from a hill, down to the river, you fell and I saw you scramble up, like thirty years before. First you wiped your knees clean, bit back your tears, and swore virtually identically—except that you now said it was our fault. We said nothing.

You could no longer cut up your own food. We saw that for the first time. You picked up your knife and fork for a moment—it seemed to be a ritual between the two of you—and then put them down again, after which my father took over and cut the potatoes and the meat into little pieces.

We heard that you could no longer take a shower by yourself. That he took you with him, lathered you and held you tight when you were frightened by the water coming out of the showerhead.

It took you about two hours to calm down when everyone arrived in the house that one of my sisters had rented. Upset by the commotion of playing children, laughter, pleasure, you went upstairs, where it was quiet. You used to be in charge, and let all that exuberant life wash over you. Now you crept away, behind my father.

She's like my shadow these days, he said.

―――――

And now you are a blue-veined china doll. You no longer wear tights but thick woollen socks. The winter bends your fingers into small, cold claws. In your footwear your toes curl against your soles. So your slow withering begins. Winter after winter you become a little more bent, you contract around yourself, under the increasingly thick sweaters and coats with which we try to keep you warm—one great vanishing point.

———

I shall have to restrain her, he says. Otherwise I'll never have a moment's rest. I can't be everywhere at once. And if she gets into the drawers and grabs for a knife or breaks a glass... She doesn't know what a knife is any more, or slivers of glass, how sharp they are. I've applied for a wheelchair from the Health Service. Then I shall restrain her, there's nothing else for it.

———————

Eventually your system will have become too weak to resist infections. A wealth of clinical terms will run riot over your bones. Your blood pressure is already beginning to drop worryingly, and you sometimes lose consciousness in your sleep. It is as if reverse birth pangs are passing through your cells and each wave is taking something else of you with it. Your insides rattle and jangle. The winter may bring the final bout of pneumonia. One day you may no longer have any appetite. You may have a fall, break something, and mess up your dislocated head even more. How far should we go to keep you alive? When does care become another word for torture?

You won't notice a thing. Whatever awareness or consciousness is still dormant in you, a frightened owl chick somewhere in the tangle of collapsed beams in your head, will glide away into the fog of morphine—we hope.

I wouldn't like her to lie there suffering later, he says.

I wouldn't want her to be dying and us to be just standing there watching.

I don't think she has to suffer.

We can arrange it, I say.

The doctor said so too. A moment will come when we all feel something has to be done.

You can't determine that moment in advance, there's no point.

But it will come, and everyone will realize: it's time.

The most probable outcome? That she'll become increasingly bedridden and one morning won't get up. That she'll sink into a coma. That she will lose still more weight, until she is all skin and bone. That her brain function will decline still further, that constant light tremors will pass through her limbs.

That her immune system will decline and she will eventually be given mush containing antibiotics. That she will lie there with the corners of her mouth twitching, that her eyeballs will tremble, that her whole body will be on the rocks.

Hopeful complications: that one day she may no longer feel any hunger. That we keep her fluid levels up, but decide no longer to feed her.

That her heart may give out, before the decline is total.

Mum, I remember I rang you the evening before you had to go in for surgery, years ago. Five top-heavy children and one miscarriage had played havoc with your body. At fifty-five you were threatening to become completely incontinent. The doctors had just come up with an ingenious system, a kind of artificial sphincter that you could operate with a button in your groin. It was to be a long procedure. Physicians from other hospitals would come and look on with fascination while you were splayed on the tilted operating table and that revolutionary technology was implanted in you.

I still wonder: is that when it began? The long period under anaesthesia? In a journal from Harvard I read, as the article puts it in clinical terms, "the formation of beta-amyloids was observed in brain cells in petri dishes to which components of the major anaesthetics were added".

I keep the article, but don't read any further.

I rang you that evening. The nurses had given you an enema, but had taken no account of the fact that you couldn't possibly retain any liquid. There was a commotion, swearing, the clatter of buckets. Everything's filthy, the floor, the sheets, you said. Call me back in a little while.

I remember thinking: if she is to be old, Death, grant her dignity. It was all so far off, I thought.

Less than ten years later there's no point any more. You've long since forgotten how to use that button. You've long since forgotten that you're a mother and I'm your son.

To the hospital with a woman who has to undergo an operation but no longer knows who she is, where she is or what will happen.

She cries like a schoolgirl on the trolley taking her to the operating theatre, calls with arms outstretched "Come, come, Dad" to my father, who watches her go with his heart breaking.

No learned spectators this time. Just the surgeon who has to undo his own work.

She comes back with a belly with rubber pipes sticking out of it and above her hip a hole from which a plastic bag hangs, which must be replaced twice a day, incorporating a pink rubber ring, which must be cleaned carefully.

In the future will I think, whenever I see an elderly lady with your posture, or with features that more or less resemble yours: you could have been like that, if you'd reached eighty-five?

How would you have grown old if the illness hadn't been there? On your side of the family there was nothing straightforward, rough or easy-going about old age. It was tough and bony. It bit on crumbling teeth, like your father and grandfather.

On father's side dying was welcomed fatalistically. To which side will I incline in old age, dying? Rather the rounded, gentle stoicism of my father, if I were to have a say in it. But do we have the choice? How great is the play between the dictates of the organism that is ours but there again not ours? How many of our decisions are conclusions based on the body, or attempts to avoid those conclusions?

I'm frightened of getting old, you said quite often, I remember, when you were in your forties. And also frightened of death, dying. Around your washbasin there was always a regiment of anti-wrinkle creams and breast-firming ointments. I should have liked to see you grow old the way your great-aunt grew old, ninety-six when she died. Smoked a fat cigar every evening and poured a stiff whisky into her body, which was the shape of a carpenter's square. At family gatherings she preferred to sit at the young people's table. Making quips and meanwhile observing all that young life with her one eye, whose vision had still not grown hazy. One evening she said that the whisky was upsetting her stomach. Before the GP could be called she was dead. Sitting up in bed, hands on her belly.

Dad felt that we should honour the dead. He took us with him to the neighbour who had been ill for so long that we thought he was showing off, but who did finally breathe his last one Saturday afternoon. We still thought he was a show-off, laid out jauntily in his Sunday suit, with his yellow-blue fingers round a rosary. He who never set foot in the church acted posthumously as a model of piety, an apparently respectable and pious gentleman, who while he was alive preferred to spend much of the day shuffling round in a grubby dressing gown, in his underwear and stocking feet. He regularly beat his four daughters black and blue until they followed his dictates, but my father said that it takes all sorts to make a world, so we went to pay our respects to the body.

He took us with him to the old man, a little way down the street, who couldn't get to the oxygen in time when he had an asthma attack. I recall—I remember—that he became a widower early, far too early, and that he always cried when Dad visited him. I had never seen an old man cry; I thought that tears dried up as you got older.

I saw Dad crying the day his mother died and all the family were called to the home and he arrived too late to say goodbye. The day after he took us to see her. In my memory he carries the three of us, my sisters and me, my brothers are too small, in his arms—but that's not possible, as I was already eleven.

You always stayed at home when we went with him to pay our respects to the dead, even then. He took my sisters and me to an outhouse behind the home, close to the laundry, where clouds of steam and the smell of soap were wafting out of the open windows. We had to wait, said a nurse, until Granny was ready, and when they brought her they had spread a purple cloth over her dress and put her glasses on.

The dead have a busy time no longer being there.

I remember being sad but not being able to cry, fascinated as I was by the phenomenal stillness of death, which I could not stand, and which had declared her body a playground for its inertia. As the years went on the fear I felt at the time cut a deep furrow in me. Mostly it stays closed, sometimes it springs open, usually at night or at sleepless moments when half-waking dreams appear and I see her lying on that bier, under that coarse purple sheet, and the razor-sharp realization hits me: she's dead. It hit me last February. Alone at home, too restless to write and not knowing where to crawl and hide, I ran the bath and it didn't help when fear kicked in with the force of a birth pang or a cramp.

I did not see your father in his coffin, or your mother. I didn't want to. I saw her a few days before her death, and we had said our goodbyes. I held his hand the evening before. The night before his death none of the three of us could get to sleep. Without knowing what the others were doing, we each got up. I sat on the sofa for hours in our dark apartment. Veerle started cleaning the kitchen cupboards, my other sister cleared out the fridge, as if we felt that "something" was about to happen. I didn't go to the laying-out. There are still dreams in which I see him on his deathbed. I bend over and have the fright of my life when he suddenly grins and waves.

When your father died, you could not be dragged away from the bed where he was laid out. During the days before the funeral you went into the room at every opportunity, appropriate or not. Normally you seldom set foot in your parents' house. I saw you several times a day sitting on the chair at the foot of the bed, or on the sofa in the corner of the room, staring at his dead body.

It's as if I've got so much still to tell him, you said.

Neighbours came and helped with addressing the envelopes for the mourning cards. Friends called to pay their respects. Gallons of coffee were poured; there was much chatter, snuffling, uproarious laughter and chat. A shame that the dead man couldn't be there himself. He would definitely have brought the gin bottle up from the cellar and refilled glasses copiously. Amid all the commotion I nevertheless wondered: what will become of us? A web of children and descendants enclosed the grandmother in her stoical grief at the head of the table. And what next, when will it be our turn? White neon light, the smell of ether, humming monitors and the nurse who comes and whispers in my or his ear: we've turned the gentleman down gently for you, if that's all right?

When she died, your mother, thirteen years later, you cried your eyes out, although the two of you had always had a difficult relationship. That's what I'm like, these days, she said. I don't know why I'm so quick to cry, I used not to be like that.

We already knew you were ill. Her emotions are becoming primary, said the doctors. Departure after departure.

Apart from your father, your sister was the only dead family member to whom we all went together to pay our respects. She was laid out in town, in a mortuary that did its dogged best not to look too cheerful, but not too depressing either. You pulled the sheet with the body under it straight, smoothed the folds with the flat of your hand and stroked your sister's forehead, with your eyes full of tears. She feels cold, so cold, just feels so cold, you kept repeating.

It's strange to observe yourself gradually starting to think about your mortality and doing so in such a sober way, as if it is part of our hidden biological clock that from a certain age you start preparing for the inevitable. Sooner or later I shall draw up the balance and I've been practising stoicism for years, which was not the strongest suit of those who went before me in death, at least on your side of the family. I saw how they clutched the sheets of their deathbeds in their fists. I, on the other hand, would prefer the covers nice and smooth when I snuff it. But in my view that is wishful thinking. We leave life behind as a half-cleared table, a desk full of papers, an unmade bed.

Life doesn't amount to much. We're born and then we die. Until about the age of thirty you are busy learning to read, write, drive and enter into human relationships that are a little more like embraces than head-on collisions, and even then we still quite regularly put the guard rail to the test. I wouldn't want to be twenty again for all the tea in China, unless a good fairy allowed me to take what I've learned with me. And even then… what have I learned? I don't know. It's more in my bones than in my language. It strikes me as improbable that you can be wise and experienced in a body that hasn't yet been through anything. Wear and tear is a form of experience. A reed that has bent a hundred times will do it more supply than a young twig that still has to learn how not to crack.

I wish I could think of you as you were, but I can't. Memories well up in us or ambush us, but they never provide us with shelter. Nostalgia does not issue from the tension between a dreamed or an imagined past and a reality that looks totally different. Nostalgia is the experience of the immense distance between between us and our recollections. Memory swiftly opens its fluid dwellings to us, so it seems, but when put into words it threatens to harden into a country house, open on Sundays from two to five, guided tours on request, please don't touch anything.

I wish that I could remember you again as the woman you were before the disease started spinning its mesh of holes in your mind, that I didn't again and again collide with that darkness, the teeth-grinding shroud of your pain and your boundless suffering.

I have a perfect picture in front of me of how she used to be, says Lieven, it's still completely intact. Perhaps because I can't bear to see her as she is now. Perhaps because I see her less. And I also think: there's no point in mourning already.

So everything must be smashed, he says.

You were the centre, you and Father. We were children and you were parents. A whole universe revolved around the two of you. Everyone was welcome. The seven of us were rarely alone for dinner. Parties in the garden, in the walled inner garden of the house where we were simply happy. Friends, boyfriends, sweethearts, lost souls in need of family affection—they were all welcome. Life, messy, exuberant, nonchalant, hard and beneficent, danced around you.

If I were a Hellenic divinity, I would transform you into two intertwined trees, with broad crowns under which on hot afternoons people could sleep, make love, read on blankets and party at tables.

But everything must be smashed.

Others who have died have strengthened me in all kinds of strange ways. With their lips that had fallen silent, before the earth covered them for ever, they quickly spelled out to me what probably matters most as long as we're breathing: that love is attention. That they are two words for the same thing. That it isn't necessary to try to clear up every typo and obscure passage that we come across when we read the other person attentively—that a human being is difficult poetry, which you must be able to listen to without always demanding clarification, and that the best thing that can happen to us is the absolution that a loved one grants us for the unjustifiable fact that we exist and drag along with us a self that has been marked and shaped by so many others.

I am afraid your slow dying, this eternal suspension between life and death, will continue to be an open wound for a long time to come. The ruin, the loss is so total. It swallows everything up. Strips you of door frames of language. Knocks window-panes from their rebates, tears the paper from your walls and scrapes the plasterwork and stones till they give way. Perhaps, perhaps a calmer land will stretch out beyond bewilderment.

I am beginning gradually to unlearn the art of hope, and as hope evaporates despair does not increase—on the contrary. Every day I wake on the edge of perplexity, the crude ore from which the new day will distil pleasure or desperation—or one of the countless alloys both contain. Growing older: getting up in the morning with permanent wounds, the stinging of which, on the way to the bidet or the breakfast table, seeks a precarious balance between despair and ecstasy. The body is again not a perfect fit. We are like adolescents, when we used to hang around angrily in the gap between our most intimate image and the image that was expected of us. Perhaps we are late adolescents: too young to be called old, too old to be young, with gout in our knees and more fragile teeth.

Later, when everything is over, I should thank my friends for the gentle Wailing Walls they erected around me, but perhaps I shall have to ask their forgiveness for all the moments when with almost voyeuristic pleasure I absorbed their bodies. The natural, worldly elegance with which they hold cups, make roll-ups, direct a ballet of pots and pans in the kitchen, and even when they are asleep they don't fall apart but their organism keeps them intact until they wake up again.

And on the bus in town, I don't look around me, I seem to be rather grazing with my eyes—sometimes I put my sunglasses on, even though there are clouds. The alarming ease with which feet negotiate steps, the toes lift the heel, the soles spring, and, going round corners, bodies regain their balance without informing us—and the way dogged nature goes on dreaming up new variations on the age-old theme of curves, arses, tits and balls, winks and quips, etcetera. I never tire of staring at it and try to smile as you sometimes used to, in those unguarded moments when a person thinks one of those countless thoughts that they share with no one: a sigh through one's nose, half mocking, half bewildered—one's own small respiratory philosophy.

What do we, basically, mean? What are we? Fluffs of seed that tickle God's intergalactic nostrils. Our existence at most makes him sneeze—his only talent for poetry. And apart from that, according to Darwin and his prophets: creatures constructed mainly of carbon, descended from an ape that one fine day fell out of its tree. Since then we have been laboriously learning to sit on the bumps, impossible to calibrate definitively. Nevertheless I am grateful to the roughly four billion years that life has folded up in our genes because the coincidence of evolution has equipped us with, among other things, mouths with blood-red stamp pads, with which we seal a host of light-footed fates, and can at least frank our tragic farces adequately.

Tomorrow we shall wake up and it will all be over. We'll hear you downstairs, at about seven in the morning, opening the cupboards and heating the kettle for coffee. We'll hear you crossing the kitchen floor in your veteran, worn-out slippers and we'll count the taps on the table top with each plate that you put down. We'll hear you moaning when the plastic round the vacuum-sealed packet of ground coffee won't budge using the scissors or your fingers, after which you'll tear it open with your teeth and spill coffee everywhere—and also the morning mood that sounds in the rattling of the cutlery and the rummaging in the cupboard when you fill our lunch boxes with bread and an apple or a piece of chocolate. We'll hear the commotion that was the medium of your stubbornness and the concern, which you could never express in subtle language, but bottled up until it spewed out as rage. Were you frightened of us? Probably you were, but equally, when the school results were disappointing or we had unsuitable sweethearts, you were probably angry at what you yourself had missed.

I threw away my own future, you said, by not giving two hoots about it at school, but you never freed yourself from the well-behaved Catholicism that you imbibed with your mother's milk. I wasn't allowed to go to art school when I was fourteen—no reproach. Too decadent, a place of free love and worse, according to the pastors for whom you cherished so much respect that every syllable that escaped them was Living Bread. And yet later, when I made my own way, you felt guilty, and were angry at your own anger back then.

Tomorrow you'll get up. You'll have put on your pink padded dressing gown and will fry eggs, and surround us with your haze of sleep and concern.

Death, let her go in a kind of forgetfulness, like one of her numerous absent-minded episodes from the past. So that without giving it a second thought she leaves life behind on the edge of the cupboard and exits the room, running her fingertips over the table top, for example one afternoon in June, when there were still poplars in front of the house and the dark grey of an approaching storm compressed the light into a bright yellow band on the horizon, behind the trunks. And then the wind getting up and the first heavy rain pattering on the leaves. And she's gone, and has long since forgotten the way back.

There is a dream that keeps recurring since you've been ill. I'm trying to find my way through a building where it is pitch-black, so dark that I am only aware of rooms that I feel my way into through the echo of my breath and my footsteps resounding from their walls, sometimes far away, sometimes nearby. Sometimes my feet bump into steps, and I pull myself up via the banisters of a staircase which leads to still other landings, other rooms and other staircases.

Sometimes I seem to be walking through long chambers, sometimes through back rooms, one after another. And everywhere the same impenetrable darkness, and everywhere the dry smell of dust, as if in an attic while the summer sun makes the tiles tick with the heat. Sometimes I feel beneath my fingers the surface of doors that will not open. And always there is that moment of gruesome realization that there is no "outside" in the dream, that I am shut up in a universe of darkness and rooms, chambers, staircases, passages and corridors that stretches out endlessly in all directions. The vast desolation of that universe, in which I am utterly alone, vomits me up out of sleep bathed in sweat.

And there is that other dream, a dream that as time goes on returns more and more frequently. I am staying with friends, family and loved ones in a house somewhere in woody hill country. It is early in the morning, a golden-yellow morning of a day at the height of summer. I walk through the house, and in the rooms hear the breathing of all those still asleep, past the table with the empty glasses and plates from the evening meal, onto a terrace, descending the steps into the garden, which slopes down to the wood. The grass gives off an overpowering smell of the earth; the sun is playing in the tops of the trees.

I sit down on a bench by a stream, suck in the air, the silence and the sounds of the sleeping life in the house. And there is always a voice that says: this is your last day. I'm not seized by fear at that moment, not even sadness. Only a yawning regret that everything will soon be over. I feel it as a bout of nausea and cramp in my jaws, deeply in love with life as I am, gruesome, majestic life.

Being ill was a kind of weightlessness when I was a child, a treat, taking leave of myself through fever and the shivers, as if I was going to evaporate. When I lay on the sofa at home racked by flu, I would wait until time shivered perceptibly through the rooms and death invariably followed at two-thirty, the time when objects lost the memory of their use. The fingerprints of their purpose slid off them and they appeared to me in a threatening nakedness, just as the worn-out things in the attic, liberated from any context, entertained each other with cheerful promiscuity and no longer cared a fig about habits.

But nothing could equal the abysmal feeling when the awareness revealed itself that it did not matter at all to objects whether I was there to see them or not. I waited for that shock, time after time, with the same mixture of rapture and terror that drove my pals towards the bumper cars at the village fair. They screamed their heads off at every collision, in something halfway between a guffaw and a cry of fear. Beneath the veils of habit objects demonstrated solemn indifference. I could sometimes be deadly jealous of their superior ability to be filled with what was absent. That ineffable privilege objects have of being not at home in themselves.

Then you would bring me glasses of diluted lemon juice, in order to tear me free, with the bitter aftertaste and the sudden assault on my taste buds, of my daily death.

We are not aware of even a tenth of the extent to which, long after the physical umbilical cord has been cut, we remain present in the membranes of our parents. Only when they disappear and die, when that alarmingly banal transition from life to death takes place in their bodies, is the last link severed. Then the weight of their fists slides from our shoulders, a weight we only feel when it is lifted.

It is a catharsis that liberates and wounds in equal measure. I feel like making music, crying languorously, rejoicing—all at once. And also cursing and hurling the kind of cries at the incomprehensibility of the universe that, equipped with more music, we used to call prayers. Nothing is unambiguous, to the extent it ever was.

It is unreal yet a fact that we can only truly reach out to our parents when they are less and less present, that the final farewell has to come before we no longer confront each other as parents and children.

If anyone had told me fifteen or twenty years ago that mourning also contains rage, seething rage, or surges of unbridled desire, I would have nodded pityingly as if listening to an obscure mathematical equation being explained by a fruitcake. The raw blessing of being knocked to and fro in the surf of longing, tumbling with the surging tide, to break on the beach, to feel the fear and sadness being pulverized. *Honi soit qui mal y pense.*

One can be too young, or at least too wet behind the ears. One can know everything but not all knowledge has already been embodied. If only there were someone who was given time, before the body turns out the lamps in all its rooms, to write down what it is, if it is only: there's not much to it. It's over just like that.

I try to tell myself—it seems to be best for everyone, not least myself—that there is no longer a person contained in that body. That when you feel in my drawers for spoons or forks or try to pull the hem of the tablecloth level with the edge of the table with your fingers, nothing more is involved than a set of reflexes, remnants of a memory of actions that flares up momentarily in your neurones.

It's easier when I write about it than when you're in front of me. My imagination, that most human of our characteristics, gets in my way, and despite everything reconstructs a personality from that battered mosaic. Then I find it difficult to think of the moment when we shall have to decide that it's enough. Then I think, though I am not religious at all: a human being has a soul.

But it may be that we need precisely that illusion to be able to let her go lovingly.

———

Were we right to keep silent with her? For as long as she could still speak, however falteringly, she never indicated that she felt there was anything seriously wrong. But what about afterwards, when language had already gone, but there may still have been some more or less lucid awareness in her mind? Should we have said: you're ill, Mum, but it doesn't matter, we're with you. You're forgetting all sorts of things, and you'll forget even more, but it doesn't matter.

Would she have wanted to give some sign? There is no answer to those questions, although they will go on gnawing at me as long as I live.

I don't believe she would ever have opted for an assisted death. When she had cancer she reacted in an oddly calm way. She seemed ready to accept that it could end badly, but fortunately it ended well.

What can make me angry is the thought that all kinds of grousers and plaster saints will find her suffering more edifying than the painful dilemmas, the struggles or the pain of those who do decide to bow out in good time—and by extension the suffering and concern of my father and his children—more virtuous then those who help and support their loved ones in their conscious decision to end their own lives. The impoverished view of morality this expresses, and the exalted way in which the grocers of suffering set themselves as prophets.

If only I could have just one look inside that head of hers. If only I could check to see if there is still "anyone" there. I was in the bath last week and heard on the radio a piece about scientists who have succeeded in talking to whales or dolphins. Even whales are more communicative than my mother now.

If I could look into her head, and someone were to say: I want to stick it out to the bitter end, I would be reassured. But if the message was: let me go, please—I wouldn't hesitate for a second, not a second.

When he drops by he leaves her sitting in the car, it would be too much fuss forcing her to get out.

How are things? I ask.

Pretty poor, he says. Very poor indeed.

When we say goodbye I see her figure behind the window glass of the car, the outline of her head, her thin shoulders.

I knock on the glass. She doesn't look up, she doesn't wave, she no longer smiles.

I have leaked out of her.

The district nurse calls in twice a day. In the morning she pulls my mother's nightdress off, washes her and helps her on with her clothes.

She also replaces the bag hanging round my mother's waist twice a day, cleans the hole in her abdomen and the rubber of the ring that keeps the bag in place.

Twice a day my mother is in a panic. When we lay her on the sofa, on her back, she grabs my forearms tightly with both hands and as we lower her there is fear in her eyes, as if we are pushing her underwater, indescribable and hardly bearable.

Keep hold of her, says the nurse, as she detaches the bag and my mother cries like a child. Are you OK? It's a bit of a shock, the smell, I know...

But I'm not shocked by the smell. I'm shocked by the sight of my mother's body: pale, emaciated. Not an ounce of fat left under her skin, her muscles sinewy and thin as threads or cables. And her sadness, her infinite sadness.

I might as well put her nappy on too, the nurse says casually. Then she can go straight to bed.

I wonder why that sentence echoes in my head for so long.

I stroke her cheek and her forehead. She calms down, and when it is all over she lies on the sofa and looks at me. Not a sweet look, but fear lying low, like our cats when there's a storm and they crawl under the table and stare at us wide-eyed, as if it's our fault.

And so that happens twice a day, again and again, because by evening the whole morning ritual is forgotten again.

We probe her like a piece of stone that has fallen from space. We take samples in search of life forms, death forms. We listen with stethoscopes to what is happening beneath her parchment surface.

She has the heart of an eighteen-year-old, say the doctors.

We push needles into the relief map of skin that her arms have become.

Her blood couldn't be better, say the doctors. All the values are normal.

It's only her muscular stiffness, say the doctors, that causes concern. But how do you get someone who's no longer aware of anything to do stretching and limbering exercises? How do you give someone who's in a constant state of panic a massage?

She must become calmer, say the doctors. Otherwise there will come a moment when she will be using more energy than she absorbs by eating and drinking.

Cardiovascular.

Intramuscular.

My mother crumbles into fragments of rock-hard Latin.

We are like a ground-control station that with all kinds of techniques is keeping a precarious satellite in orbit around the earth—but for how much longer?

Every morning at about ten, except for Mondays, he takes her in the car to the home where she can receive day care. He could also have her collected by a minibus, the dementia bus, which every day bumps its way along the country roads for miles around, carrying its load of superannuated schoolchildren, but he doesn't want to, and I understand him. He takes her in the car. He only accompanies her as far as the entrance. He stops at the sluice gate that screens off the area where she is from the exit.

One of the old ladies, who is also in day care, recognizes her and pulls up a chair for her by the big window. And so that's where she sits. The nurses have asked me if they can pop her in the bath on Tuesday.

That's all right by me.

At home it's impossible to get her into the shower any longer. It seems that hot water calms her down.

That she still responds when the nurse calls her name.

My godchild comes to visit. He goes into the garden with his younger brother in search of skulls and bones from the black-birds and pigeons that cats have caught. Their father and I drink white wine, and talk about life, about loss, about the life urge that in unguarded moments translates into raw pleasure, singing hunger. He lost his father early.

It releases you from a life predicated on the future, which doesn't exist yet anyway.

We drink in silence; there are always enough pearls of wisdom.

His sons come back in. My godson has found the skull of a wood pigeon and one of a rat and empty snail shells. He holds the fragile bones up to the light and looks in fascination at the curves in the gossamer-thin bone.

I can see the little globes where their brains were, he says.

He is all eyes, my father, in the square in front of the cathedral and the theatre.

I haven't been in town for at least five years, he says.

While we were parking, the disabled card lying on the dashboard caught my eye. I turned it over and suddenly saw a photo of her, taken when she was still well.

Her broad smile, her bright-eyed look. And the pride in her make-up.

I turned the card over again quickly. Seeing her as she was before the illness struck is unbearable. The way she looks today is equally unbearable.

We hang motionless, impotent, between what we don't want to remember and what we can't bear to see.

In the restaurant he says: I've acted stronger than I am. And too often I've unburdened myself with An.

I say: no one expects you to be strong. No one expects you to be able to handle this.

It's quite something, he says, leaving someone behind whom you've known for fifty years.

You're not leaving her behind. No one expects you to be her nurse. You're entrusting her care to others, so that you can be there for her better.

The waitress comes and refills our glasses. Father and son? she asks. I thought so. I do that regularly, go out for a meal with my son. Then for all I care the rest can be blown sky-high.

Precious moments, she says.

We smile.

I think: everything's already been blown sky-high.

———

In the past, whenever I wanted to give her a kiss, a sheet of blotting paper always came between us.

Child of parents who were ashamed. Of themselves, of history, of what people thought. The affection which a granny would generally have expressed with all her limbs in cuddling her grandchildren was put by her mother into the cakes she baked for us on birthdays. Pleasure palaces of flaky pastry, whipped cream, biscuit and chocolate. Whenever we had flu her father would stand snivelling by our sickbeds, because each time anew he thought our last hour had struck. Thoroughly nice man, but never affectionate.

When they gave us pocket money for the summer fair, they couldn't help adding: don't waste the money. What they meant was: make sure that we don't have to be even more ashamed.

My mother, daughter of shame.

Always that clumsy, half-mocking laugh when I tried to press my lips on her cheek. For a long time I cursed that shame, which she mixed in with our food, and its shadow side, self-reproach.

Now I lift her up out of the chair in the day-care centre. Veerle releases the table top and I lift her up.

Her feet thrash against my shins, and when I let her down she perches jauntily on my toes.

She is restless, as almost always these days. She wants to run in all directions at once. Until Veerle says: we're going home, Mum. Home to Dad.

She calms down instantly. She more or less flops against me, with her head against my ribcage. I hear her breathing calming, I feel it in the threads of my shirt.

I give her a fond kiss on the forehead.

———

We've been expecting you for some time, says the lady from admissions, after offering my sister and me a chair in her office. But we don't force anything. We never do that. The request must come from the family.

I saw also that your father was completely at the end of his tether.

The man had no strength at all left. Nothing left.

It still affects me to see a grown man, twenty years older than me, cry. Believe me.

He had absolutely no reserves left, your father.

Of course he felt guilty.

I said: we'll try it for a week or so. Then we'll see.

Now he realizes it's the right thing too. For him too. But if she is admitted permanently in a little while, it will all come back.

There will always be guilt feelings, believe me.

―――――

She likes walking, your mother. Group activities are not for her. But she likes stepping out.

So every day, weather permitting, one of the duty staff goes walking with her.

We also put her in the multi-sensory bath. We close the curtains. The nurses light pleasantly scented candles, because you have to keep stimulating people with dementia. Especially pleasant, direct sensory stimuli.

That relaxes her.

As long as she can walk, your mother.

So everything there is, I always say, is still there.

———

If she moves in here permanently she'll be put in a family group. We don't believe in leaving people with dementia sitting in their rooms. If you had to sit looking at four walls, you might not be so happy either.

We have a movement therapist here, we ensure that our guests don't stiffen up. And there are ergotherapists. Yes, there are still lots of things you can do together with people with dementia. In short bursts, depending on their ability to concentrate.

Sometimes there is cooking in the unit. The smell of fresh vegetable soup often makes them curious. Some lend a hand in chopping up the vegetables. Others don't. We won't be able to do it with your mother. But, anyway, if she's there, she's sure to pick up on the life around her.

I sometimes come into the unit when they're cooking and tend to get angry because nothing is happening. Because the guests are not responding.

But then the therapists say: that's what you think.

Smelling, they say, sniffing the smell of fresh soup, is also doing something.

We throw parties regularly here. It may be that when you come to visit her the central entrance hall is closed off and you have to enter by the side door. For example a couple of times a year we organize a marathon walk. We follow a route round the park.

It's touching to see how much they enjoy it. There is still a group feeling among those people, however ill they may be. It's natural, just as with us, and you should see their pleasure when they reach the finish line all together.

Then we close off the big entrance hall and give a party with drinks and snacks.

That's the right way, I think.

Parties are important.

Don't forget that.

―――――

Your mother is at present in category C/D. That is the highest grade. Needs constant care, and has dementia.

It's a miracle that all of you and your father have held out for so long.

I'll admit her as soon as there's a place free. We have a hundred and sixty-two beds. We're completely full, and there's a long waiting list.

It's not as nice working here as when I started thirty years ago.

Then I had perhaps forty admissions a year to arrange. That was always a pleasure. Now I have a hundred and thirty per year. I have to disappoint a lot of people.

It's a huge problem. I sometimes wonder whether our politicians realize.

But I do what I can.

———

We go to collect her, my sister and I. In the day room she is sitting in her chair by the window. She constantly purses her lips and relaxes them again.

At a table a group of elderly ladies are playing cards.

A man says: don't you live in H.?

I grew up there.

On what side of the tracks ?

The right side.

He giggles.

———

Do you know what persuaded me most? asks Veerle, after we have hoisted her into the back seat of the car together.

No, I say.

At least it doesn't smell of stale piss in there...

When I look at her, an unreal grimace cutting right across her mouth mocks me to my face. Impulses pass through nerve cells, playing on the muscles like puppets. I think of a fen in summer, half hidden in the shade of foliage. Green water. Now and then a gas bubble wells up. Leaves rot. A carp breaks the surface and gasps for breath.

Shortly, when she leaves for good. Shortly, when she is helped across the threshold (perhaps by us, her sons). When we have packed her case (her daughters, probably). When we open the gate for her, the door of the car, and someone takes hold of her under the shoulders and someone else lifts up her legs into the seat…

Will he then, our father, have to close the door behind her and turn the key?

I don't know if I want to see her shuffling across the gravel, where the orchard used to be—one of my earliest memories: I am lying with her on a blanket and I'm sucking on the shells of freshly picked peas. The taste explosion of the raw green on my tongue, still as sharp as ever when I think back.

There were newborn lambs dancing around us.

It must have been the spring of 1966. Is it possible that I am remembering this, or is it one of the snatches of memory of someone else that roamed around there under that roof in the extensive firmament of memories in my earliest years?

I have at home a medallion of Napoleon III, which supposedly once belonged to her great-grandmother, and which when I was small was kept on "their side" of the house, the side where my great-grandfather, her grandfather, lived.

With the children of my brothers and sisters the house has reached its fifth generation, probably the last.

My grandfather was laid out on the bed in which he was conceived.

There were ghosts in the attic, ghosts with boots on.

The war is over.

They smell empty, the rooms upstairs. Of my childhood when the forefathers had left the house and this world. It suddenly smells of their clothes again and their breath and their chewing tobacco, of the linoleum that used to cover the floorboards. Of the dust in the dull yellow curtains. They stayed away for years, those olfactory ghosts. Now they are freeing themselves from the pores in the walls, and moving outwards with great intensity.

The smell of autumn decay, when out the bedroom window the light of the street lamp, a bulb under a porcelain cap, jangled to and fro in the wind. Farmer De Poorter collected the household rubbish with his horse and cart in the middle of the night. In stormy weather he sheltered under his cart, by the horse, which stood stoically on the verge while the lightning flashed.

Awakened by the wind, the jangling street lamp, by horse's hooves on the asphalt, by the cosmic thundering. One night lightning struck nearby. All the fuses blew, and the sockets spewed little blue flames. Farmer De Poorter called "Gee up! Gee up!" to his horse, which had sparks flying out of its hooves. In the sand of the garden path there was a gaping crater with glass walls where the lightning had struck.

These are images that are more bat-like than memories. They detach themselves from the beams from which they were hanging upside down asleep and flutter through the night. And the ancient dead in their shrouds of rain and autumn air, wood and plaster ooze from the walls.

One day they will absorb her too, and later emit her again: as the sour smell that hides in her clothes, the body odour of her bitter fears.

I can remember her voice, but not her words. Sometimes her laugh echoes through my dreams or my semi-waking slumber. That animal pleasure of hers in the past when the house or the garden was full of people and the delight with which, as soon as the first warm spring sun shone, she stretched out naked in the deckchair, behind the cherry laurel.

In the past, I say.

It's good to have friends on your sofa now and then and to watch them leafing through albums. Then I can look through their eyes at photos which otherwise cut me too deeply with their sharp edges.

I remember, years ago, sitting with Lieven on the old railway embankment looking out over the marshes near the River Lys in the evening sun. We were sitting on the embankment, in the tall grass. In front of us the soggy meadows, the rows of trees. Behind us the town and its hum. It must have been July. I remember that the hemlock had finished blooming.

Lieven said: look, there go your parents.

They were walking on the far bank of a wide canal, at the foot of the dyke, behind the reeds and the bulrushes, under the lancet-shaped leaves of the silver willows. He a little behind her, she looking around her with pleasure in the calm evening light. She was wearing a wide white dress that swayed in folds around her knees. They did not see us.

I wanted to call out something, but Lieven said: leave them be. Look how happy they are. And I felt a great sadness as I saw them vanish among the leaves.

I remember.

I remember the blue plastic child's bathtub on the table in the front room. I remember the texture of the blue-and-white check flannel, on my tongue and my lips, while I am sitting in the bath—the assault on my taste buds, the sour flavour of soap.

I remember, she and her sister have wrapped me in the towel, I remember the cold of the floor under my feet.

I remember her saying later: fancy you remembering that. You'd only just learned to walk.

I remember the house, still empty without brothers and sisters, and me crawling towards her between the blocks and toy cars across the black-and-white tiled floor. She is wearing a black leotard because in the afternoons she does gymnastics on a rush mat. I crawl towards her, and she looks down at me with amusement. I sit down on her feet, which she moves up and down under my bottom. I bob and rock and laugh out loud.

I don't remember any other expressions of tenderness from her, except much later.

I remember the small scullery where one afternoon the first washing machine she bought, no more than a drum in white enamel, alarmed me when the centrifuge started up, as if the appliance were irritated by my presence. I remember her banjo which hung vibrating on a hook above it.

I can't remember ever hearing her play on that banjo.

I remember her crying, one afternoon on the sofa in the empty house, and not knowing why.

I remember my younger sister in a purple bikini riding circuits on her tricycle round the paving stones of the back garden. And also the intense green of the lawn, and the grey ribbon of the dead-straight garden path.

I remember the faint jangling of the springs on the pram in which my youngest sister is sleeping, over the gravel of the country road under the poplars while we are on our way somewhere; perhaps we are just going for a walk, perhaps we are on our way to one of her friends. I remember that she has put white socks and sandals on my other sister and me, and that the socks go grey from the dust on the country road. She has placed a couple of locks of hair over her cheekbones and is wearing that summer dress with stylized poppies and buttercups.

Sometimes I remember the wind which blew in gusts through the tops of the trembling poplars and wrapped the house in the soft rush of leaves. Safety.

But I also remember nights so quiet that the silence seemed to congeal into whispering in the darkest darkness imaginable. And sometimes it was her voice, sometimes his, when they talked in bed, softly, so as not to wake us. If they were quarrelling her voice sounded more abrupt, cutting, his more plaintive, deeper. From her I imbibed the poison of reproach, from him I inherited fatalism. During the day she soon started shouting when they quarrelled. And he shouted back. They were sometimes frightening, for a child, those moments of verbal thunder. Only later did we understand why it often got so loud: they didn't know how to quarrel. They shouted in frustration at not being able not to love each other.

I remember her having words with my sisters during their adolescence. Mothers and daughters. Could she do anything but repeat the difficult love of her parents with us? I remember the argument in the conservatory, the broken glass when she and my younger sister stood shouting and pushing each other on one side of the door. They both cut themselves, not only literally, and afterwards licked their wounds, not only figuratively. How many legacies do we bequeath to the innocent creatures who merely want to love us, weighed down with rucksacks of their own, with their load of bread and cobblestones?

I remember the embarrassment and later the amused mockery when we could hear them making love. The bang when the leg of their bed gave way. And how afterwards, I don't know for how long, it was propped up by my father's thick crossword dictionaries, before a new one arrived.

They bought furniture that was virtually falling apart. Five children had to be able to play indoors too, not stuck sitting as good as gold on the cushions on which the slightest smudge or stain would spell humiliation. We converted the living room table into a galleon, and in the twilight area beneath the dining table made our own house, our own family. My sisters were mother, the youngest brothers the babies. Why did I always have to be the dog? With knitting yarn we wove intricate labyrinths, crazy spider's webs from the chandeliers to the door handles to the feet of cupboards and chairs. She gave us our head, but she was ashamed if we, when there were posh visitors and she asked us to lay the coffee table, quite simply lifted the door of the cutlery cupboard off its hinges, because they had so often served, those doors, as a raft or a shield that they clattered onto the floor at the slightest touch. I am still amazed at the toughness of chairs, their dogged, creaking endurance. Even under the most ponderous bums they held out, much to our disappointment.

I remember her rust-coloured corduroy trousers with the orange back pockets. Her pancake trousers, the trousers she always wore when she was going to make pancakes in the evening. I remember we waited for those trousers like Druids waiting for the solstice.

Love is gravity.

I remember all of us in their bed, us five and our parents, on Saturday mornings. Making mountains with the blankets. Bedouin tents of linen. Pillow fights. My father lifts my youngest brother up by his shins. We cart books and pillows and toys along with us: a litter of five naked mice and their parents, on a Saturday morning long after ten.

When she was in the maternity clinic we were allowed to sleep with him in turn in the big bed, the bed where we must have trickled from him into her. Sometimes I stayed awake to experience the protective presence of his body for longer. The whole room was permeated with safety and warmth. We were jealous, the nights when it wasn't our turn, but we felt safe just the same.

For me love needn't be more than a hospitable kind of indifference, a spot, a house, a garden, his belly when he sleeps or lies reading, where behind hedges or walls, or in the soft hollow between his ribcage and pelvis, I find shelter from the simultaneity of everything and everyone. Places, in short, where I can dispense with the imposed pride of constantly being myself.

I remember her telling us about her boarding school days in Wallonia, where her parents sent her because she was a hopeless case. She had to go to a boarding school in Le Roeulx, with an order of nuns in a convent endowed by the family of the Princes de Croy, whose scions lived an invisible life in their château full of peeling gold leaf and commodes with turned legs, right next to the boarding school.

I remember her telling us about one particular nun who passed through the cloister every morning in her nightdress and each time bowed humbly to the life-sized crucified Christ on one of the walls—while each time her pee spilled over the edge of her chamber pot. And I remember the stories about that other nun with whom she regularly had to share a bed, especially in the winter months, against the cold. At home, she also told us, her sister always got angry because in the winter months she would press her icicle-like feet into her sister's warm back.

She only held out for one school year. In the holidays she hitch-hiked home. She got lifts from the lorries laden with coal from the mines around Charleroi. She would throw her case in the back with the shiny anthracite and chat with the drivers in the cab.

Freedom.

―――――

We are not sovereign beings. We are like fragments of the earth's crust, the thin, grinding shell around the world, dented under the pressure of the other lives around us. For large distances serrated. Here and there as flat as a pancake. Sometimes rounded and slippery.

She is now a glacial valley—an ice field has scraped over her, and the earth has been scoured away by the masses of ice. In the bare stone, wide furrows are legible. Every relief has been smoothed flat.

If we hold up her coat for her to put on, she immediately walks the other way.

If we hold the left slipper ready to put on, she lifts her right foot.

Still our mother, says An.
Still just as stubborn.

We give her a send-off like parents do when their child goes to their first summer camp. Handkerchiefs are never far away. In her case are the things we have chosen. Material that we hope will extend like an umbilical cord between the place where she will be staying and the house where she spent her childhood and has seen her own children grow up. We know she'll never return, and that we mustn't expect postcards.

In time the years when she was ill, the years of drudgery, misery, will not so much fade away as, finally, become simply one particular period in her and our existence. Then she won't be just this grinding, trembling, collapsing body that is dying at a snail's pace. Memory, elastic and creative, will stretch over the gaping wound, the silent toothless mouth of her suffering, a stretchable membrane of stories, a safety net. I know there will be holes in it. For years there will always be one moment every day when we push through that protective skin and are temporarily helpless—my father at least. That's how it goes, I know. I am frightened of that loss, or rather I accept it just as toothache goes with having teeth—very reluctantly.

She won't fade, but will crystallize further into a host of facets. We will understand her better as we ourselves experience the stages of life that she has also experienced, and we will, too late, draw resigned conclusions and grant her forgiveness. That's how it goes, I know.

Finally we shall enter the phase of life when she no longer grows along with us—unless we undergo the same fate.

Soon there will be grandchildren who will absorb her into their story universe in the form of snatches of narrative and snaps and a gravestone—like me, who just under fifty years ago bathed ignorantly in the murky amniotic fluid of so many ancestors. For the other grandchildren, who are older, life will fill the empty space she leaves behind with other treetops in the great human wood.

After us she will become static as an ancestral statue and slowly dissolve in the rush of time. When all's said and done, what do I know about, say, my great-grandfather, who died when I wasn't yet four? His voice, rasping, but no words. His weathered hands, which he always held on his back whenever he took always the same walk with An and me down the same country road. His bald pate sticking out above the sheets on his deathbed. His shadowed profile, in the permanently darkened half of the house where he lived with his wife, and, after her death, alone. Every quarter of an hour a Big Ben clock sent a touch of Albion chasing round the dark living room. Their wedding photo hung on the wall in an oval frame with plaster wreaths of flowers.

And yet he is still "there", in me, as a kind of nebula, a constellation of images, impressions, sounds, smells and stories handed down by others. Time does not unite us in oblivion but unravels us into memories. I only started writing properly, I suspect, when I began to realize that words are at their best when I can make them vibrate like minute compass needles in response to those elusive magnetic fields that constitute someone's whole "being"—rather like the way iron filings form patterns on a sheet of paper under which a magnet is held. From the cloud that my mother is becoming and that in fact she already is, slivers of images will shoot out unexpectedly, strangely sharp—the way she laughed, the gesture with which she arranged a lock of hair behind her ear... And then we will say: yes, that's how she was.

Every year at the approach of winter she became restless. She began rattling the saucepans louder than usual. More washing-up broke in the washing-up bowl than outside it. We were apprehensive of the impatience smouldering in her. Her hands were looser, slaps flew all around. We were never really afraid of her ticking us off: too half-hearted, too soft.

She started taking long walks through the fields, to sniff the smell of the potato tops that had been set on fire. A smell that, like no other, reminded her of autumn. Then when we came home from school the bread was on the table, untouched in its paper bag, the jam, the sugar, the milk and the coffee in the thermos taken from cupboards and trestle tables and hastily put on the table in scattered array, and she was gone. It was a regular pattern. The overcast October skies, the first storm. The mysterious departure of the swallows reminded us that her wintry summer was beginning.

The winter was her spiritual high season, a feast of chilliness that I share with her. It's best if it freezes your socks off. The branches of the trees must sway stiffly to and fro in the wind. Everything must be tight, fixed in the crystal silence, and the light must be pale and bony and reflect my sadness and impossible longings. When it's freezing I think of the dead and sons I shall never have, however much I spin them round in the summer of my imagination, throw them in the air and catch them. My sons, who will never grow taller than me, and will never hear the sighing in the bare branches, of the wind perhaps, the freezing cold, or the lame voice, the blue lips of the father I am not.

I remember her jealousy watching the figure skating championships on the first television we owned, a humming black-and-white box with a capricious character which sent us from channel to channel entirely as it pleased. The news gave way without any prior announcement to a fuzzy trapeze act in some Russian circus, followed by a drink-sodden Slav in a precarious imitation of Edith Piaf. The thing was connected to a wobbly aerial in the attic. The Belgian channel had the best reception when the aerial was reinforced by the winter coat of my late great-grandmother, which we hung, coat hook and all, from one of those steel antennae. The reception of foreign stations, besides being heavily dependent on the weather and the ancestral wardrobe, was greatly influenced by the number of pigeons squabbling or copulating in the gutter.

She watched the figure skating in a state of trance-like concentration. There was a hint of *Schadenfreude* in the sigh of disappointment with which she greeted a fall.

If it froze for long enough, she unearthed her skates from a dusty box at the bottom of the wardrobe. She got out her bike. She tied the skates to the carrier and disappeared. She took the same route I took as a child, when I biked to school, through the woods.

The woods were a different world, a good counterweight to the mindless atmosphere I have encountered in all the classrooms in my life. The woods were rampant; they disseminated the smell of excess, a tangle of survival and decay. The local, half-senile baron had neglected logging for years. The woods had closed ranks. The dead-straight avenues laid out by enlightened squires two centuries before to introduce order and rhythm into nature had gradually become completely overgrown. Here and there the contours of an antique amphora on a moss-covered pedestal betrayed the point where several avenues had once converged. The château farms were some way off the road in a disorderly fringe of overgrown bushes against the edge of the woods, surrounded by a few plots of orderliness. In the summer cocks crowed in the farmyards. Pigeons circled above the cultivated fields.

Slightly less than two hundred metres further on, the woods gave way to the bank of an extensive stretch of water. As a child she came here to swim with the children of the tenant farmers without realizing that her forefathers had dug out this hole in the ground spade by spade to extract peat during the famine years in the mid nineteenth century. In order to combine usefulness and pleasure the baron had the workers pile up the earth they had dug out in three mounds. On one of them he built his pleasure garden. The other mounds were surrounded by water and planted with trees.

She always forbade us to swim there, because of the boggy ground. In digging out the layer of peat an underwater current was exposed that could carry swimmers away with it. In the winter too she was on her guard. She would wait till three or so skaters were flashing over the surface of the ice before she left the bank and made for her favourite spot: a broad creek cut off from the rest of the pond by a long dam between one of the islands and the grounds of the country house. The trees by the water's edge were pock-marked with age. They spread their gouty branches across the water. Almost no one would disturb her there. Most skaters thought that the bay belonged to the country house. No one would spy on her.

First she skated in big circles. She took a run-up, suddenly made a sharp turn and then spun a few times around her own axis, until she fell over.

She always fell. Once, when I was with her, the surface of the ice creaked ominously. I pressed flat against the ice with arms and legs outstretched, like her. I could hear the cracks creeping farther for a number of seconds. I felt like a fly in a huge, chaotic web of fault lines.

Bad ice doesn't creak, our father always said, she said. It swallows you up without a sound. Good ice has to settle.

Don't worry about that creaking.

It will go out gently, he says.
It will all go out gently.
And then she won't recognize me any more either.

———

Last night I dreamed that it had snowed heavily and was very cold, a frosty night, and that she wanted to play outside, in her nightdress. She danced through the garden barefoot in the snow, and hid in a hollow tree trunk. She wanted to sleep, she said, and there was no moving her, while it got colder and darker.

I heard someone, perhaps my father, say that she no longer had any awareness of cold or time, and it might be best if we let her sleep. We went inside and left her behind.

In the morning I went into the garden. The snow had receded. It was an early spring day. Between the bare tree trunks and the blooming, shining-white wood anemones I saw children who seemed at once very young and ancient romping over the paths. They cooed and screamed and had identical white dressing gowns on. One of them danced past me exuberantly and mumbled something. I knew it was my mother.

I saw her disappear into the undergrowth with those other children, heard their laughter fading and I thought: it's for the best.

PUSHKIN PRESS

Pushkin Press was founded in 1997, and publishes novels, essays, memoirs, children's books—everything from timeless classics to the urgent and contemporary.

Our books represent exciting, high-quality writing from around the world: we publish some of the twentieth century's most widely acclaimed, brilliant authors such as Stefan Zweig, Marcel Aymé, Antal Szerb, Paul Morand and Yasushi Inoue, as well as compelling and award-winning contemporary writers, including Andrés Neuman, Edith Pearlman and Ryu Murakami.

Pushkin Press publishes the world's best stories, to be read and read again. Here are just some of the titles from our long and varied list. For more amazing stories, visit www.pushkinpress.com.

THE SPECTRE OF ALEXANDER WOLF
GAITO GAZDANOV
'A mesmerising work of literature' Antony Beevor

BINOCULAR VISION
EDITH PEARLMAN
'A genius of the short story' Mark Lawson, *Guardian*

TRAVELLER OF THE CENTURY
ANDRÉS NEUMAN
'A beautiful, accomplished novel: as ambitious as it is generous, as moving as it is smart' Juan Gabriel Vásquez, *Guardian*

BEWARE OF PITY
STEFAN ZWEIG
'Zweig's fictional masterpiece' *Guardian*

THE WORLD OF YESTERDAY
STEFAN ZWEIG

'*The World of Yesterday* is one of the greatest memoirs of the twentieth century, as perfect in its evocation of the world Zweig loved, as it is in its portrayal of how that world was destroyed' David Hare

JOURNEY BY MOONLIGHT
ANTAL SZERB

'Just divine… makes you imagine the author has had private access to your own soul' Nicholas Lezard, *Guardian*

BONITA AVENUE
PETER BUWALDA

'One wild ride: a swirling helix of a family saga… a new writer as toe-curling as early Roth, as roomy as Franzen and as caustic as Houellebecq' *Sunday Telegraph*

THE PARROTS
FILIPPO BOLOGNA

'A five-star satire on literary vanity… a wonderful, surprising novel' *Metro*

I WAS JACK MORTIMER
ALEXANDER LERNET-HOLENIA

'Terrific… a truly clever, rather wonderful book that both plays with and defies genre' Eileen Battersby, *Irish Times*

SONG FOR AN APPROACHING STORM
PETER FRÖBERG IDLING

'Beautifully evocative… a must-read novel' *Daily Mail*

THE RABBIT BACK LITERATURE SOCIETY
PASI ILMARI JÄÄSKELÄINEN

'Wonderfully knotty… a very grown-up fantasy masquerading as quirky fable. Unexpected, thrilling and absurd' *Sunday Telegraph*

RED LOVE: THE STORY OF AN EAST GERMAN FAMILY
MAXIM LEO

'Beautiful and supremely touching… an unbearably poignant description of a world that no longer exists' *Sunday Telegraph*

THE BREAK
PIETRO GROSSI

'Small and perfectly formed... reaching its end leaves the reader desirous to start all over again' *Independent*

FROM THE FATHERLAND, WITH LOVE
RYU MURAKAMI

'If Haruki is The Beatles of Japanese literature, Ryu is its Rolling Stones' David Pilling

BUTTERFLIES IN NOVEMBER
AUÐUR AVA ÓLAFSDÓTTIR

'A funny, moving and occasionally bizarre exploration of life's upheavals and reversals' *Financial Times*

BARCELONA SHADOWS
MARC PASTOR

'As gruesome as it is gripping... the writing is extraordinarily vivid... Highly recommended' *Independent*

THE LAST DAYS
LAURENT SEKSIK

'Mesmerising... Seksik's portrait of Zweig's final months is dignified and tender' *Financial Times*

BY BLOOD
ELLEN ULLMAN

'Delicious and intriguing' *Daily Telegraph*

WHILE THE GODS WERE SLEEPING
ERWIN MORTIER

'A monumental, phenomenal book' *De Morgen*

THE BRETHREN
ROBERT MERLE

'A master of the historical novel' *Guardian*